# A Left-Handed History of the World

## Ed Wright

PIER **9**

First published in 2007 by Pier 9, an imprint of Murdoch Books Pty Limited

Murdoch Books Australia
Pier 8/9
23 Hickson Road
Millers Point NSW 2000
Phone: +61 (0) 2 8220 2000
Fax: +61 (0) 2 8220 2558
www.murdochbooks.com.au

Murdoch Books UK Limited
Erico House, 6th Floor
93–99 Upper Richmond Road
Putney, London SW15 2TG
Phone: +44 (0) 20 8785 5995
Fax: +44 (0) 20 8785 5985
www.murdochbooks.co.uk

Chief Executive: Juliet Rogers
Publishing Director: Kay Scarlett

Commissioning Editor: Hazel Flynn
Project Manager: Colette Vella
Editor and Photo Researcher: Ariana Klepac
Concept and Design: Peter Long
Production Controller: Maiya Levitch

Text and design copyright © Murdoch Books Pty Limited 2007
All images copyright © Getty Images, with the exception of images on pages 136 and 142 which are copyright
© APL/Corbis.

9781741960532

PRINTED IN CHINA.

# Contents

# *Introduction*

TAKE A GOOD LOOK AT THE TABLE OF CONTENTS IN THIS BOOK AND TRY to imagine what the world would have been like if these great lefties had never lived. Try to imagine the Italian Renaissance without Leonardo, Michelangelo and Raphael, science without Isaac Newton or Marie Curie, the American novel without Mark Twain, the computer without Alan Turing or Bill Gates, baseball without the Babe. And that's before we even begin to consider the left-handed statesmen, soldiers, rulers and conquerors whose effect upon the shape of history has been so enormous.

Left-handers have a disproportionate presence in the history of the world. Looking at the table of contents, you could be forgiven for thinking they would have been cherished throughout history as a source of special gifts and insights. But sadly, despite all they have brought to human progress, this is mostly not true. Throughout history, left-handers have been discriminated against. They have been burned as witches, refused as marriage partners, had their hands tied behind their backs when they tried to write with the left hand, and beaten into orthodoxy. Faced with these obstacles, many lefties have submitted, and have spent their lives trying to pass as righties, which makes the achievement of the people in these pages even more impressive.

Discrimination against the left-hander is one of the deepest prejudices there is. The proto-Indo European language, spoken before 3000 BC, and from which ancient languages such as Sanskrit, Greek and Latin as well as most European vernaculars are derived, had a word for "right," but not one for "left," apparently because of the taboos associated with that side of the body. When subsequent languages developed a word for left, the connotations were usually appalling. In Latin, the word for left is *sinistre*, from which our word "sinister" is derived, while the word for right is *dexter* from which we get dextrous. In Greek, *skaios* means both left-handed and ill-omened or awkward. In Hindi, following the proto-Indo European, left hand is *Ulta Haanth*, which simply means the wrong hand, while in French,

it is *gauche*, which has crossed over into English with the meaning of clumsy, especially in social circumstances. The word for right in French is *droit* which also means law. In German, it's worse: *recht* means right-handed, the law and also correct, while *links* means both left-handed and weak. In English, people are right and have rights, while others are left behind. The etymology of "left" is from the Friesian (a region on the North Sea Coast of Holland and Germany) *luf* meaning weak and worthless, while the Old English *lyft* once combined with *ädl*, meaning disease, to form the word for paralysis. It's no wonder then that left-handers are more likely than their right-handed friends to be dyslexic. This also may be part of the reason why so many of the great left-handers have starred in non-linguistic domains, such as math, sciences, technology and the visual arts.

Around 10 percent of the population is left-handed. This seems to be fairly constant across history and culture although, in places where discrimination against the left-hander is particularly strong (in the conformist culture of Japan, for example, which reports five percent of the population as left-handed), people are less likely to own up to left-handedness, while many natural lefties will buckle under the pressure and switch. Given the historical discrimination against lefties in virtually all cultures (the ancient Incas, who thought left-handers lucky, were an exception), it's hard to know how many great lefties are missing to history, their handedness switched, concealed or not recorded at all and thus assumed to be right. While the figure is around 10 percent of the population, men—of whom 12 percent are lefties are 50 percent more likely to be left-handed than women, of whom only 8 percent are lefties. One theory for this is that left-handedness is caused by the exposure of the fetus to excess testosterone in the womb.

Left-handers tend to be nature's risk-takers. This is also perhaps why left-handers have a disproportionate presence in the annals of human achievement: they take more risks, and sometimes they pull them off. It might be the physical risk of battle, found in lefties such as Alexander the Great or Napoleon; or intellectual risks, as in the case of philosopher Friedrich Nietzsche, who found that when he looked into the abyss of meaning, it looked back at him. Historically, these kinds of risk-taking have tended to be more of a male preserve, which makes the short career of Joan of Arc so spectacular. Possibly this is because males are not as vital to the perpetuation of society. Perhaps it's because for women, childbirth is enough of a risk in itself.

In the primate family, only humans are restricted to 10 percent left-handers, and there is no conclusive evidence to suggest why. Other members of the primate family can be left- or right-handed, the ratio is roughly equal. It has been suggested that right-handed dominance has something to do with the way language is run from the left hemisphere of the brain. Another possible explanation is that the development of more intricate tools—scissors, for instance—privileged one hand over the other. It does, however, seem likely that this proportion has remained fairly constant throughout the history of humankind. But why? One theory that has arisen to explain this is that left-handers have ensured their evolutionary survival by the advantage of surprise in hand-to-hand combat. Put simply, most people expect to be attacked with the right hand and are not as competent in defending themselves against the left. If too many people become left-handed, however, then this advantage of the unexpected would obviously be diminished.

To a certain extent this theory can be used to explain the disproportionate presence of left-handed players in sports such as tennis, baseball and cricket. The play of a left-hander is more difficult to predict because the angles are different. It can also be argued that if left-handers have enjoyed this advantage in a physical sense, their minds have evolved to maintain it in a mental or abstract sense. In other words, the left-hander's ability to surprise is not just limited to hand-to-hand combat or sports. This can be seen in the careers of people like Alexander the Great or Napoleon, left-handed military geniuses who profited by their power to outwit the enemy through surprising strategies on the battlefield. Furthermore, it can be said that this capacity of the left-hander to use surprise translates to the deployment of unorthodox stratagems in other areas of life. As the philosopher Walter Benjamin once said, "All the decisive blows are struck left-handed." Many, if not all, of the great left-handers in this book have made unorthodox moves. They have been agents of major changes that have astonished and transformed their worlds and altered the course of human history.

You may have heard the expression, "Only left-handers are in their right minds." This is because the left side of the body is controlled by the right-side of the brain. In neurological terms, left-handers tend to be what is termed "right-hemisphere dominant." Studies have shown that the right and left hemispheres of the brain perform different cognitive functions.

The right hemisphere, for instance, has primary responsibility for managing the visual and spatial aspects of sensory perception. Architecture, for example, is a profession renowned for having a large number of left-handers. Possessing enhanced visual and spatial faculties can be an asset in fields ranging from the visual arts (Leonardo, Michelangelo and Raphael), industrial design (Henry Ford), sports (Babe Ruth, Martina Navratilova and John McEnroe), or on the battlefield (Napoleon, for instance, who had an amazing ability to visualize maps). This faculty is also connected to the ability for abstract visualization that often generates mathematical genius. More than a quarter of the people featured in this book were brilliant at math: Leonardo, Newton, Napoleon, Carroll, Curie, Turing and Gates. Another link often conjectured is one between mathematical thought and music. Recent research into phenomena such as synesthesia has shown that both these gifts may be related to an enhanced visual-spatial faculty in the mind. It is no surprise then that many of the great left-handers featured here are scientists, visual artists, mathematicians and musicians.

The hemispheric functioning of the brain, however, is more complex than simply right and left dominant. This is particularly the case with

MANY, IF NOT ALL, OF THE GREAT LEFT-HANDERS IN THIS BOOK HAVE MADE UNORTHODOX MOVES. THEY HAVE BEEN AGENTS OF MAJOR CHANGES THAT HAVE SURPRISED AND TRANSFORMED THEIR WORLDS AND ALTERED THE COURSE OF HUMAN HISTORY.

left-handers. As Chris McManus argues in his book, *Right Hand, Left Hand,* while almost all right-handers have the same type of left-hemispheric dominance, the situation with left-handers is more diverse. For example, while 95 percent of right-handers have language dominance in the left hemisphere, only 70 percent of left-handers do. McManus argues that left-handers, on average, have greater cerebral variability than right-handers. In other words, lefties are risk-takers in neurological terms too. The brains of left-handers have a built-in tendency to be different: more reason why they can be expected to be harbingers of change and disturbers of the status quo.

This innate difference of left-handers is accentuated by the fact that they have to operate in a world that doesn't fit them. Some, frustrated by the dictates of society, become rebels, while others seek sanctuary by devoting their genius to largely solitary pursuits, where their unique minds are allowed to reign free. Other left-handers, however, adapt to a world where things are often the wrong way round. While this may be an impediment in the operation of can openers, scissors and circular saws, it means that the left-hander's mind is more fully trained in adaptation than the right-hander's. We learn through imitating those around us. Most of us learn by imitating right-handers. For a lefty, this learning demands translation or adaptation; an extra cognitive step. Lefties have to concentrate harder to work out what to do. Perhaps this is the reason why there are so many left-handed actors. This extra step may also be the generator for the lateral thinking found so often in the left-handers in this book.

## TRAITS AND EXPLANATIONS LIST

In analyzing the personalities and achievements of the great lefties, some traits seem to stand out as being left-handed. Not all the subjects have them but, as you will see in individual chapters, each of the lefties here has a combination of them. In many cases the latent talent is brought out and amplified by the circumstances of individual life. These traits are not exclusive to lefties, but these left-handers have been gifted with them to a prodigious extent. They are also suggestive rather than conclusive. As you read this left-handed history of the world, look to the lefty links in the margins and you will see obvious and surprising connections between the various protagonists, as well as information about many of the other great lefties who have shaped our destiny.

INTUITIVE There seems to be a special kind of intuition, an awareness that shows in the reading of situations and the solution of problems. It's an ability to leap through the stages of conventional thought to penetrate to the core of a question and come up with unexpected answers that surprise those around them. Sometimes it's a battle tactic (Alexander), other times it's a deep affinity with mathematical structures (Newton), or the ability to rewire the received wisdom on a subject in an unorthodox but effective

OPPOSITE: TENNIS PLAYER MARTINA NAVRATILOVA, WINNER OF 18 GRAND SLAM SINGLES TITLES AND 40 DOUBLES TITLES.

manner (Ford). Left-handed intuition can also be the result of that extra step in the lefty's learning process; the necessity of having to adapt right-handed information produces an enhanced awareness of the self.

**EMPATHETIC** While some left-handers turn their intuition toward themselves, or abstract it into mathematical or musical terrains, others use it to achieve a knowledge of others. This skill is often found in the kind of left-hander who tries to join the hierarchies of right-handed society. Alexander had it when he wanted to, as did Julius Caesar. Bill Clinton is another lefty renowned for it, as was Charlie Chaplin. Often this empathy can be camouflage for the ruthless ambition lurking beneath.

**VISUAL-SPATIAL ABILITY** With the right hemisphere of the brain usually dominant, in terms of visual-spatial perception, great left-handers are often vested with superior skills in this area. As I have argued above, this ability is also related to having gifts for mathematics and music. Perhaps the most neurological of all the lefty traits, this ability has artistic, scientific and military applications.

**LATERAL THINKING** Lateral thinking is the ability to make unortho-dox connections. It also has the quality of metaphor; being able to see one thing in terms of another. We have seen that left-handers' brains have more variety in the way they are wired. It can also be argued then that left-handers have more variety in the ways that they think. This ability to see one thing in terms of another is evidenced by the way Isaac Newton, for instance, could visualize the general movement of heavenly bodies in the action of an apple falling from a tree in an orchard. Or how Alexander could look at his men's leather tents and transform them into a flotilla of rafts that enabled his army to cross a river and conquer the opposition.

Two kinds of lateral thinking stand out strongly as markers of left-handed genius: adaptive and transformational. The first is based in the necessity of adapting and learning how to operate in a right-handed world. This means that the left-hander can often have a chameleon-like quality, an ability to change as circumstances demand. Transformational thinking is perhaps an emphasized version of this gift. These types of lateral thinking are, for instance, one reason why so many actors are left-handed, since the ability to become someone else begins with mimicry then becomes self-transformation.

On another level, the desire for transformation is enhanced by the fact that the left-hander exists in a world that doesn't quite fit them. At its most extreme this manifests itself as the creative-destructive impetus of compul-sive conquerors such as Alexander or Napoleon, who seize control and then embark on the impossible quest of remaking the world. It can be said that the left-hander is innately an agent of change. Indeed it may even be our evolutionary function in terms of the survival of the species.

OPPOSITE: LUDWIG VAN BEETHOVEN COMPOSED SOME OF THE WORLD'S GREATEST MUSICAL WORKS, DESPITE BEING STONE DEAF FOR MUCH OF HIS LIFE.

**HOT-TEMPERED** There's no use trying to hide it. Many left-handers have ferocious tempers. From Alexander to Super Brat John McEnroe, the whole spectrum of anger is on show from childish tantrums and bravery in battle to cold-blooded fury. It may have something to do with the discrimination lefties face in life, or the extra obstacles they have to overcome. Or it may have something to do with the theory that the genes for left-handedness can be triggered by exposure to excess testosterone in the womb.

**SOLITARY** One approach, when you don't fit in, is to pretend as much as possible that the rest of the world doesn't exist. Beethoven, Nietzsche, Michelangelo, Newton, Turing, Carroll and Joan of Arc all belong to the category of lefty solitaries, while others such as Leonardo and Bill Gates show a tendency.

**ICONOCLASTIC** As argued above, great left-handers are innately agents of change, who eschew traditions and laws and march to the beat of their own lefty drum. Many left-handers abhor the confinement of social or intellectual structures and thus derive satisfaction from knocking them down so their own individuality has space to flourish.

**SELF-TAUGHT** If you ever thought flunking school would be the end of you, then this book will help you to think again. Some of the greatest minds in history showed little aptitude in their schooling while others, such as Alan Turing, got in trouble for ignoring the curriculum in favor of more complex mathematics. Still others, such as Mark Twain, Henry Ford, Joan of Arc and Charlie Chaplin, hardly had an education at all. What many of them do have in common, though, is an emphasis on learning by doing, rather than through reading books. Experience is valued above theory. This trait can be found in Leonardo's attitude to nature, Marie Curie's preference for experiments over theory, Mark Twain's use of real American speech in his books and Jimi Hendrix's guitar playing, to name but a few.

**EXPERIMENTAL** A combination of the iconoclastic, experiential, self-teaching and lateral thinking aspects of the left-hander, rather than observing the rules, these left-handers operate on the principle, "What if …?" then try it out. This trait is linked to the left-hander's inborn tendency to operate as an agent of change.

**FANTASIST** The variability of the lefty mind can be a hit and miss affair. Uniqueness in itself is no guarantee of success. Not all conceivable changes exist within the realm of possibility. However, what is possible changes from generation to generation, and left-handers, with their powers of seeing beyond the status quo, are often at the cutting edge of making the seemingly impossible come true. In other cases, fantasy provides a mirror for looking at ourselves: it is literally the left hand looking at the right.

OPPOSITE: FOUR OF THE LAST SEVEN US PRESIDENTS HAVE BEEN LEFTIES, INCLUDING THE 42ND US PRESIDENT, BILL CLINTON, WHO SERVED FROM 1993–2001.

# Ramses the Great

EGYPT HAD 13 PHARAOHS BY THE NAME OF RAMSES, BUT ONLY THE left-handed, redheaded Ramses II is remembered as Ramses the Great. Taking over from his father, Seti I, in 1279 BC, this pharaoh of the nineteenth Dynasty fought bravely against the Hittites, most notably at the famous battle of Kadesh, and expanded the territory of the Nile Kingdom. With the Hittites, Ramses also concluded the world's first recorded peace treaty, which bore many of the similar conditions seen in modern counterparts. His 67-year reign was phenomenal, given that the average lifespan of an Egyptian at the time was 30–40 years, and the consequent political stability brought enormous prosperity to the Nile Kingdom. With this wealth Ramses built some of the most amazing monuments known to all antiquity. He also managed to sire an enormous number of children—between 100 and 400—to the many wives in his harem. Because he lived to such an old age, many of Ramses' children pre-deceased him. It was his thirteenth son, Merenptah, who eventually inherited the throne. Ramses' reputation as a great pharaoh has endured for thousands of years. In 1976, when his mummy was taken from Egypt to Paris to be treated for fungal growth, it was met by a full French military guard of honor at the airport.

**EARLY RAMSES** Ramses II was the third of the nineteenth Dynasty pharaohs whose origins were from Egypt's military elite. The dynasty was founded when the last Pharaoh of the eighteenth Dynasty, Horemheb, who had no sons of his own, chose his military commander, Ramses I, as his successor. One of the reasons he did this was because Ramses I had a son, Seti, who could in his turn take over, thus enhancing the stability of the regime. Ramses I only lasted two years before his son, who was co-regent, took over. Following in the family tradition, Seti introduced his son Ramses II to military life from an early age. According to the hieroglyphs—and it must be remembered that the official records of the

Ancient Egyptians were prone to boasting—Ramses II showed considerable prowess on the battlefield and was a military commander by the age of 10. When he was 14, Seti appointed him co-regent and when Seti died in 1279 BC Ramses, still in his early twenties, became Pharaoh.

**KING RAMSES II** From the outset Ramses was a proactive Pharaoh. One of the first challenges he faced was the incursions of the Shardana sea pirates (from the coast of Turkey) who were causing major problems for Egypt's Mediterranean trade. In only the second year of his reign, Ramses cleverly placed his navy, backed up by troops, at strategic positions along Egypt's Mediterranean coast. He allowed the pirates to attack, drawing them into a false sense of security. Then he counter-attacked and the pirates were completely surprised. After capturing them, Ramses showed typically left-handed lateral thinking. Instead of slaughtering the pirates or sending them off to work in the harsh slavery of the Nubian gold mines, he incorporated them into his own army (presumably their wives and children were held hostage to assure loyalty) where their straight swords, horned helmets and round shields proved a significant asset in a number of battles, including Kadesh. In the next few years of his reign, Ramses proved a smart military strategist by building a series of forts (next to wells and thus self-sustaining) northwest of modern Alexandria to protect Egypt from bands of Libyan marauders whose influence in the region was growing.

**BATTLE OF KADESH** The most famous battle of Ramses' military career was undoubtedly the Battle of Kadesh and it illustrated both the advantages and disadvantages of the Pharaoh's mercurial left-handed temper. Early in his reign, Seti had made some strong territorial gains in Syria, at the expense of the Hittites who were based in Turkey. However, by the time Seti died, the Hittites had regained this territory, including the prized city-state of Amurru (in Lebanon) and the fortified hill town of Kadesh (in Syria) where much treasure was kept.

In the fifth year of his reign, Ramses set out with an army of 20,000 men, split into four divisions—named after the Egyptian gods Amun, Re, Ptah and Seth—to recapture this territory. They marched up the coast of Canaan and through the Bekaa Valley in southern Syria, approaching Kadesh from the south. As they approached Kadesh, the Egyptian Army discovered two Bedouins lurking about who, when questioned, informed Ramses that the army of the Hittite King, Muwatallis, was still about 120 miles to the north. Thinking he had gained the advantage, Ramses set off with his Amun division toward Kadesh. Not expecting to encounter significant opposition, the other three divisions lagged behind as Ramses and his elite division raced off to set up camp on the northwestern edge of the city.

Unfortunately for Ramses the rush of blood associated with his hot, left-handed temper prevailed over his strategic intuition—a feature of left-handed military leaders throughout history. Shortly after Ramses and his division pitched camp, Ramses' forces captured a further two Hittite spies. The truth that was beaten out of them revealed that the first two spies had been plants designed to trick Ramses into a false sense of security. The Hittite army, numbering around 37,000 soldiers, was hiding behind Kadesh, ready to launch a surprise attack. Ramses urgently tried to get word to his other divisions and sent the non-combatant parts of the expedition, including a number of his wives, away to safety.

The warning came too late. As the Re division approached the royal camp, they were attacked and virtually decimated by 2,500 of the famously formidable Hittite chariots. Having broken the Egyptian line, the chariots then turned toward the Egyptian camp and Amun division fell into serious disarray. At this point things looked bleak for the Egyptians. It was likely that Ramses would become the first Egyptian pharaoh to be captured in battle: a major disgrace. But rather than submit to this, Ramses mounted his chariot and led his household troops in a series of counter-charges that confounded the Hittites, who were already counting the spoils of victory. Ramses fought fiercely, inspiring his troops, who were further aided by the arrival of troops from the Syrian coast, including the former Shardana sea pirates. The Hittites, surprised by the ferocity of these attacks, fell into disarray and those who weren't slaughtered were forced to swim across the Orontes River to where the main part of the army was camped in relative safety. The two armies ceased fighting for the evening and by the time they lined up against each other the next day, it seemed the only possible result would be a stalemate after much bloodshed. A truce was declared. Even though Ramses had been out-strategized, his bravery and the divine fury of his left-handed rage on the battlefield saved the day against an army almost twice the size of his own. However, it must also be noted that he had failed in his chief objective of capturing Kadesh.

**PEACE TREATY** After Kadesh, an uneasy peace reigned between Egypt and the Hittites until the death of the Hittite King, Muwatallis. Muwatallis' youngest son, Mursili III, inherited the throne, but was unpopular and only managed to reign for seven years before he was deposed by his uncle Hattusili III. Mursili was exiled to Syria, then Cyprus, before seeking refuge at the Egyptian court, where he tried to cause as much mischief as possible for his uncle. Ramses refused Hattusili's repeated requests for his nephew's extradition. For a while it looked as though war between the two empires was going to break out as a result. However, the military resources of both countries were concerned with more pressing campaigns, involving actual territory rather than pride: the Egyptians were fighting against the Libyans and the Hittites against the Assyrians. Instead of war, diplomats for both sides met over a period of two years and the result was the world's first known peace treaty.

When we think that the Egyptian and Hittite empires were fighting over territory which today belongs to Israel, Lebanon and Syria, the ability to abandon enmity in favor of peace seems extremely impressive, given that

 **LEFTY LINKS**

1. Ramses II conquered the Shardana sea pirates then incorporated them into his army. The pirates who encountered Julius Caesar, another formidable left-hander of the ancient world, were not so fortunate. After being captured by them, then released upon payment of a ransom, Julius Caesar tracked them down to their island lair, defeated them, took their treasure and had them all executed.

2. A similar kind of hot-tempered desperation to Ramses' behavior at the Battle of Kadesh was shown by Joan of Arc. Against the odds, she led her army by inspiration to victory at Orleans. However, the next time she attempted this she was captured and handed over to the English, who set in motion the processes which led to her being burned at the stake.

3. After he signed the peace treaty with the Hittites, Ramses reigned for a further 46 years, a period predominantly marked by prosperity and peace. Although he had a strong martial streak in his personality, Ramses tempered it in order to achieve harmony and wealth for his land. As such, his reign bears considerable resemblance to the nineteenth-century British monarch Queen Victoria, who loved a good war but reigned through mainly peaceful prosperity for 63 years.

4. Ramses II belonged to the very exclusive club of being a left-handed redhead. Other members include Napoleon I, Nicole Kidman, Robert Redford, Mark Twain, John (Johnny Rotten) Lydon and possibly the King of the Franks and Holy Roman Emperor, Charlemagne.

## RAMSES' LEFTY TRAITS

**LATERAL THINKING** Ramses' capacity for lateral thinking is evidenced by his involvement in the world's first known formal peace treaty. Also, his strategy of claiming the monumental glories of previous pharaohs by changing the inscriptions and defacing the statues to take on his own image can be considered lateral—a sign of the left-hander's innate facility for transformation.

**HOT-TEMPERED** This seems to be Ramses' defining left-handed trait. It is reflected in his battle strategy, and in his rashness and haste when building his prosperity.

**ICONOCLASTIC** This lefty trait is most notable in Ramses' tendency to disfigure statues of previous pharaohs and change their likenesses and inscriptions to his own. A number of his temples are also notable for the fact that his statues have been carved on the same scale as the gods. Even though all the pharaohs were divine, this was still a departure from the norm.

**EXPERIMENTAL** Ramses experimented with peace treaties, new modes of building monuments as well as military strategies such as the system of forts he built across the northwest borders where the Libyan tribes were a threat.

PREVIOUS PAGES: FOUR COLOSSAL STATUES OF RAMSES AT THE ENTRANCE TO THE GREAT TEMPLE OF ABU SIMBEL.

OPPOSITE: DEPICTION OF KING RAMSES II OFFERING TO THE GOD RA, FROM THE INTERIOR OF THE TEMPLE OF ABU SIMBEL.

this is a region of the world that holds long grudges and seems obsessed with the notion of "an eye for an eye." It took considerable lateral thinking from the two kings to come up with a document that, despite continuing tensions between the two nations, enabled them to co-exist peacefully for the next 40 years of Ramses II's reign.

The treaty consisted of 18 articles. The first article was a non-aggression pact. The next two established a mutual alliance that either party would go to the aid of the other in the face of invasion by a third power. A further three articles promised that the kings would go to each other's aid, or their sons' aid, should there be an internal attempt to overthrow the crown or its intended heir. The next 10 articles constituted the world's first extradition treaty, whereby fugitives from one regime would not be allowed to live in the other; rather they would be captured, treated civilly and then handed back to their place of origin and whatever fate awaited them. The final two articles cited the authority of 1,000 gods from both countries as witnesses, guarantors of the treaty and sanction against breaking it:

> They who do not observe the words that are in this silver tablet, the great gods of the country of Egypt as well as the great gods of the country of Hatti will exterminate their houses, their country and their servants.

Although Egypt was forced to give up its claims to Kadesh and Amurru, the treaty established a valuable right of travel and trade for Egyptians within the Hittite territories, giving them free access to the Mediterranean port of Ugarit. The terms of peace were highly advantageous to the ensuing prosperity of Ramses II's reign, more so than if Ramses had persisted in his attempts to acquire Hittite territories. This is an example of lateral thinking on the part of Ramses.

The peace wasn't always easy, however. To begin with, the continued presence of Mursili in Egypt was problematic: the Hittites believed the extradition treaty should be retrospective, while Ramses did not. After Ramses had sent prized Egyptian doctors to the Hittites he complained that he had only received one lame servant in return. Yet 13 years after the treaty had been signed it was reinforced when the Hittite king offered one of his beautiful daughters to Ramses, who developed such a taste for them (and their sizeable dowries), that he married two more. The royal wedding strengthened the treaty considerably so that when a king of Asia Minor, Mira, approached Ramses in the hope of forming an alliance against the Hittites, Ramses rebuffed him saying, "Today there is fraternity between the great King of Egypt and the King of Hatti …"

**MAN OF MONUMENTS** One of the main activities of an Egyptian pharaoh was the building of monuments. Because he was Pharaoh for over 60 years, Ramses built many of them. Part of the reason why he remains so well known to history is because of the sheer weight of the monuments he left behind. Yet curiously, even though his presence in the ruins is large

compared to most pharaohs, much of the construction was shabby and the masonry wasn't nearly as fine as in the reign of his father, Seti. The left-handed temper and rashness that saw Ramses deceived and isolated from his troops at the Battle of Kadesh also seemed to be at work in Ramses' attitude toward his monuments. Like Alexander the Great, Ramses the Great was a man on a mission in a hurry—perhaps because he had no reason to expect to live as long as he did. Also, it took a long time to build monuments and, for this reason, Egyptian pharaohs generally began building their tombs as soon as they were throned. For Ramses, the urge to monumentalize himself was insatiable. In his reign, he not only constructed some of the greatest monuments in antiquity, but an entire capital city, Piramses, which was, unsurprisingly, named after himself.

Egyptologists frequently note that, for Ramses, it was case of quantity over quality. In order to make possible his lust for monuments, he made extensive use of the slave labor he captured in his military campaigns. For the inscriptions and images in his temples, Ramses traded in the delicate and time-consuming raised relief—whereby images were lifted clear of the background—for the much quicker process of sunken relief, where the images were carved into the stone. Another reason for the adoption of this technique was that it was harder to change an image once it had been carved. Ramses had good reason to think of this. Not only was he a prolific builder, he was also a repurposer of monuments built by pharoahs who had gone before him. Again, this kind of shortcut displays the predisposition for impatience that went with his hot-headed, left-handed temperament. One of his tricks was to get his stonemasons to work on statues of his predecessors, chipping away at them until the statued ended up being an image of Ramses instead. This is about as close to the concrete definition of iconoclastic as you can get.

In other areas of self-immortalization, Ramses showed a willingness to experiment. His most striking monuments include the twin temples dedicated to Ramses and his favorite wife, Nefretari, at Abu Simbel on the banks of the Nile, near the border between Egypt and Nubia. The most extraordinary feature of the temple was the four enormous statues of himself. Ramses used the unusual technique of carving these directly into the cliff face as opposed to the imported slabs of granite which were usually the material for such endeavors. Each one was over 65 feet high and the whole complex took more than 20 years to build. It was an experiment which had a lasting effect. The statues at Abu Simbel would become the inspiration for the statues of great American presidents carved into the rock at Mount Rushmore, which were also roughly the same size as those of Ramses built 3,000 years earlier. Despite Ramses' reputation for hasty workmanship, many of the works he commissioned are still identifiable today.

OPPOSITE: ONE CAN STILL SEE THE BASIC FEATURES OF RAMSES THE GREAT FROM LOOKING AT HIS MUMMY, WHICH WAS DISCOVERED IN 1871 AND IS NOW PRESERVED IN CAIRO'S EGYPTIAN MUSEUM.

# Alexander the Great

356–323 BC

SHORT AND LEFT-HANDED BUT IMMENSELY STRONG, BOTH PHYSICALLY and mentally, Alexander the Great is probably the most formidable conqueror and most charismatic warrior statesman the world has ever seen. A great hand-to-hand fighter and master military technician, his political decisions were often strikingly original. Between his coronation as King of Macedonia at the age of 20 and his death at the age of 32, he acquired control over an unparalleled domain, which stretched from Afghanistan, India and Uzbekistan in the east, through Iran (then Persia), Iraq, Kuwait, (Mesopotamia), Syria, Egypt, Turkey, Bulgaria (Thrace), and breached the Danube in the north. In his own times, he was king of over half the known world, stretching over 2 million square miles. His army fought for 12 years without losing a battle. It marched over 20,000 miles and defeated adversaries with much larger armies and killed more than 200,000 enemy soldiers and 250,000 civilians.

One of Alexander's most significant weapons was the original angles produced by his brilliant and ruthless left-handed mind. While bravery and unity were important, the ability to outthink the enemy was perhaps Alexander's greatest talent. Wherever he went, he left people bewildered to the extent that, throughout the Middle East, he almost ceased being considered a human, becoming a force of nature whose terrifying brilliance is still invoked in bogeyman tales used to frighten children into obedience, while his Macedonian compatriots considered him not just a king, but a god.

**EARLY ALEXANDER** Alexander's ability to see what others didn't was crucial to his success and reputation from a very early age. A famous instance of his burgeoning prowess, recorded by the eyewitness Marsyas of Macedon, was Alexander's taming of the horse, Bucephalas. The horse had been sold to Alexander's father, Philip, King of Macedonia, who became angry when Bucephalas proved to be wild and unmanageable, and

A DETAIL VIEW OF A GOLD MEDAL SHOWING ALEXANDER THE GREAT WEARING AN ELEPHANT SCALP. ALEXANDER MADE HIS PUSH INTO THE INDIAN SUBCONTINENT IN 326 BC.

allowed none of his men to mount him. When Philip ordered the horse taken away, Alexander interjected, "They cannot handle him because they lack understanding and courage," and demanded the chance to ride the horse himself. Philip initially didn't respond to his son, but Alexander persisted until he asked him, "If you do not manage him, what price will you pay for your rashness?" Alexander responded that he would pay his father the price of the horse and, amid much laughter from the King's companions, Philip assented to the wager. He had already lost. Alexander had noticed that the reason Bucephalas was so unwieldy was because he had become spooked by having his own shadow in front of him. He turned the horse around so he was facing the sun and encouraged him gently before taking a flying leap and mounting him. When Philip noticed his son's success he allegedly said, "My boy, seek a kingdom to match yourself. Macedonia is not large enough to hold you." While it was a brave thing to mount the horse, it was Alexander's ability to see things differently from everyone else, his capacity to get under the skin of the horse and intuit what was bothering it, that proved the deciding factor.

The tale of taming Bucephalas, while showing Alexander's bravery and brilliance, is primarily one of empathy. It's a quality more commonly associated with women than men. However, empathy is a faculty often concentrated in lefties. Why? The dissonance between lefties' sense of themselves and their surroundings often has the psychological effect of causing alienation. Because of this the lefty has to learn how to adapt more than the righty. This involves learning the thinking of people (or horses) who think differently to oneself, in the same way perhaps that a migrant develops knowledge when trying to adapt to a new society. This capacity for empathy, born from alienation, is what enabled Alexander to solve a problem that his father's best horsemen couldn't. It would also give him a powerful political advantage over the Persians, in places such as Egypt and Babylon, because he understood and was tolerant toward their local religions and, through this, managed to bring their inhabitants onside. Alexander's ability to escape the prejudices of his own culture was undoubtedly helped by the fact that, unlike many of the left-handers in these pages, Alexander had one of the best educations anyone could hope for. His personal tutor was the great philosopher, Aristotle, who complemented his physical prowess with strategical smarts and insight into the human condition.

PREVIOUS PAGE: BY THE END OF HIS 11-YEAR REIGN, AT 32 YEARS OF AGE, ALEXANDER HAD BECOME RULER OF HALF THE KNOWN WORLD.

## GETTING ONE OVER THE GETAE

Few battles illustrate the unorthodox genius of Alexander's practical thinking as clearly as his victory over the Getae at the Danube. With his father Philip's assassination in 336 BC, Alexander became King of Macedonia at the age of 20. His ultimate ambition was to take on the Persians, but he had the foresight to realize that if he embarked on such a long-distance mission, it was necessary to annihilate all of Macedonia's neighboring threats first. After quelling internal Macedonian dissent, he headed north into Thrace (modern day Bulgaria), vanquishing the Triballian and Illryian peoples who had revolted when they heard of the death of Philip. When chasing the remnants of their armies, he found himself on the southern shores of the River Danube in present day Romania. Across the river were the Getae, a tribe of sun-worshippers who had allied themselves with Alexander's enemies. They'd known of Alexander's approach for weeks and had assembled a large army—around 4,000 cavalry and 10,000 infantry—to repel any Macedonian attempt to cross the river.

The Getae were used to defending their turf: over the years they'd repelled invasions by a range of marauders including Scythians, Persians and Celts. They were confident that Alexander would take time to get across the Danube because, from their experience, the usual solution was to build a bridge. All they had to do was wait and attack the point where Alexander attempted to do this. With the combination of a strong force and the river against him, the Getae thought Alexander would be sensible, and consider the Danube as the natural limit of his campaign. If he didn't, they were confident that much of his army would be fish food by the time they got across. All they had to do was wait and see which option he took.

Alexander was in a quandary. The more he looked at the river and the Getae army on the opposite shore, the more he wanted to cross it and defeat them. The obvious answer was to build a bridge, but he knew that if he did that the chances of defeat were high. The stakes were high too. If a second-rate military power like the Getae were proved able to defeat him, he would lose the aura of invincibility he was acquiring, and that would make his passage into Asia to defeat the Persians far more difficult.

Perhaps he should turn around. They were fairly close to the Black Sea, and the Danube, having flowed over 1,500 miles from its German origins, had grown wide. More importantly, Alexander's men, coming from the mountainous regions of Macedonia, couldn't swim.

Still, there had to be another way. One thing Alexander had noticed was that along the banks of the river were a number of canoes which the locals used mainly for fishing. He sent his men out to requisition every one they could find. However, when they came back it soon became clear that although the boats were useful, there simply weren't enough of them to get the army across in sufficient numbers to take on 14,000 Getae.

It wasn't looking promising and most military leaders in this position would have given up. Not Alexander. Now he had seen the Danube, he needed

☞ LEFTY LINKS

1. Alexander's tutor was the great philosopher Aristotle. In various sources it has been asserted that Aristotle was also left-handed. However, the evidence is inconclusive.

2. As with many left-handers, direct evidence for Alexander's left-handedness is difficult to find. Handedness has rarely been remarked upon in history. The Hebrew *Book of Jossippon*, however, mentions Alexander talking of the superiority of the left hand and of how "kings stemming from the tribe of kings are left-handed."

3. The rage which powered Alexander's path of conquest, and was also the seed of his destruction, fits the model of the Dionysian principle, as expounded by the left-handed philosopher Friedrich Nietzsche.

## ALEXANDER'S LEFTY TRAITS

**INTUITIVE** Alexander's passage of conquest and mode of battle were largely intuitive endeavors.

**EMPATHETIC** Alexander was able to empathize with his soldiers which, for the most part, earned him their loyalty. He was also understanding of other cultures, and even of his horse.

**VISUAL-SPATIAL ABILITY** This skill was particularly necessary in the planning and execution of battle plans, especially those involving hand-to-hand combat.

**LATERAL THINKING** Alexander had this in spades, and it was primarily this quality that enabled him to continually outwit his enemies. His transformative capacity to see his army's tents as potential river-crossing vessels against the Getae was crucial to the victory, as well as the reputation he began to accumulate throughout the Ancient World.

**HOT-TEMPERED** Alexander had a combination of the left-handed and Balkan propensity for violent rage. In one incident he killed his friend Clitus with a spear after a drunken quarrel. In January 332, the citizens of Tyre, in what is now Lebanon, offered to surrender to Alexander, but their religion didn't allow him to sacrifice in their temple. Enraged, Alexander decided to lay siege to the town. When his troops forced their way into the city, they slaughtered 6,000 troops. Alexander then ordered that 2,000 civilians be crucified on the beach.

**EXPERIMENTAL** Alexander experimented with new tactics in battle. Yet he was also interested in social experiments. For instance, he tried to blend Greek and Persian society through intermarriage and put troops from different races together in his army. In addition to carnage, he also founded more than 70 cities, including Alexandria in Egypt which, with its famous library, was to become the cultural capital of the Ancient World.

PREVIOUS PAGES: PAINTING BY JEAN-SIMON BERTHELEMY OF ALEXANDER THE GREAT CUTTING THE GORDIAN KNOT.

to cross it. It was part of the incessant drive within him, a combination of curiosity and conquest. With dusk approaching, and a decision yet to be made, his army began to unpack their tents for the night.

As he walked among his men while they were setting up their tents, Alexander got an idea. Macedonian tents of the day were made from leather, and leather was waterproof. What if you sealed a tent . . . better still, filled it with straw and sealed it watertight? Would it float? If Alexander's men hadn't revered him so completely—when he took a tent and stuffed it with straw, then told one of his men to see if he could float on it in the river—they might have mutinied. Instead, that night, through the genius of their commander and his army's faith in him, the Macedonians safely crossed the river, unknown to the Getae, via a scraped-together assortment of canoes and tents.

Alexander had chosen a deep cornfield to land in, which gave the Macedonians excellent cover. Early the next morning, he sent his troops in to attack. The Getae were so amazed that Alexander had managed to cross the great river without building a bridge that they scattered on the first cavalry charge. The Macedonians chased them toward their town. Instead of defending it, the Getae gathered their women and children, then fled. Alexander decided to let his army plunder the town. He then ruthlessly razed it to the ground, so it could no longer be used as a focal point for further revolt.

Alexander's victory of the Getae was a classic case of conquering the enemy with the power of the unexpected. In an era without radar, combustion engines, aerial reconnaissance or long-range artillery—let alone guided missiles—one furthermore beholden to omens, portents and the capricious wills of multiple deities, the power of surprise cannot be underestimated. But how was this surprise achieved? And what might it have to do with lefty thinking?

**ALEXANDER THE GREAT LEFTY** Today's left-handers know that the world hasn't been designed for their use. Every time they pick up a pair of scissors or a can-opener they have to adapt them. Whereas a right-hander feels things to be natural, that the world has been created to fit their needs, for the lefty, experience has a permanent dissonance. While this can be annoying, in creative terms, it's a bonus. At one level, the lefty is always translating the world, and from this constant activity of translation comes the desire to transform it.

These forces were clearly at work in Alexander's defeat of the Getae. To begin with, he won the battle because he refused to bow to the accepted wisdom that a bridge was needed. Left-handers have less investment in the status quo because it simply hasn't been designed for them. In Alexander's case, this attitude grew to become one of the hallmarks of his character. His encounter with the philosopher, Diogenes the Cynic, is a classic example. Diogenes was famous for his indifference toward the collective vanity of society. When Alexander, as ruler of most of the known world, asked Diogenes what he could do for him, Diogenes told him he could stop blocking his sunlight. Alexander was so impressed by this lack of respect for the status quo that he replied that if he hadn't been Alexander, he would have liked to have been Diogenes—the unkempt philosopher, who in today's society would be categorized as a bum.

Lacking respect for the status quo is perhaps why a higher proportion of lefties end up in prison but, when combined with daring and talent, it sparks originality, something Alexander had in spades. In the battle against the Getae, the most obvious manifestation of this originality is the use of tents stuffed with straw to float his men across the Danube. This adaptation of something to suit a new purpose for which it wasn't designed, belongs to the same branch of thinking as the lefty's perpetual challenge of reorienting and translating the world. The primal scene of the lefty's realization that the world doesn't fit, generates a powerful motivation to alter and invent things. By adapting a familiar object for an unfamiliar purpose, Alexander was able to have his men in position to surprise the Getae when they charged out from the cornfield that morning. The transformation of tents into rafts, something only Alexander visualized, was the pivotal moment in the victory.

**LEFT RIGHT OUT** Alexander's original goal was to conquer Persia and revenge the injury to the Greeks of the Persian King Xerxes' invasion some 150 years before. In October 331 BC, Alexander succeeded when he defeated Darius, King of Persia, at the Battle of Gaugamela, with enormous cost of life to both sides. Darius fled back to the capital, Persepolis, where Alexander crowned himself King of the Persians for the first time. He acquired so much treasure that it took 500 camels and more than 2,000 pairs of mules to carry it out. He also captured Darius' wife, universally considered the most beautiful woman in the Persian kingdom, and was able, if he so chose, to assemble the most ravishing personal harem the world had ever known. Xerxes' magnificent palace was also his to inhabit and, with the Persians' talent for luxury renowned, he could have lived a life which most people could only dream about.

Yet Alexander's dreams were of a different order. Instead of enjoying the spoils of victory, he got drunk one night with his friends and gave them permission to burn Xerxes' palace to the ground. He then spent the next five years camped out in some of the most inhospitable regions of the world, such as Afghanistan, in preparation for battle with whatever army happened to venture into his orbit. In the process he would alienate himself from his most loyal comrades, watch many of his soldiers die, kill his best friend with own hand, stain his brilliance with paranoia and essentially conquer his way into an early grave. Why?

While the story of Bucephalas illustrates how the lefty's alienation is capable of inspiring empathy, it can also inculcate a special kind of rage, an unquenchable fire of anger leveled almost against being itself. The rightness of the world we know is an arbitrary thing. There is no good reason why a left-oriented world wouldn't work just as well. Intelligent lefties feel this keenly. It's frustrating: their limbs work perfectly well, yet they are stigmatized, because the right-handers, knowing the groundlessness of their advantage, have historically resorted to the kind of wrong-headed discrimination evidenced by the characterization of the lefty as evil and clumsy in languages all over the world.

It is indubitable that Alexander suffered from this rage. Warfare provides an outlet in which this kind of rage becomes a celebrated activity. It takes a remarkable amount of energy to try to conquer the

A ROMAN MOSAIC DEPICTING ALEXANDER THE GREAT ENGAGED IN BATTLE WITH DARIUS III, KING OF PERSIA (IN THE CHARIOT), AT ISSUS.

world, because why would someone bother if they actually liked it? Alexander needed enemies to feed his rage. Whenever he stopped fighting, his rage would inevitably begin to eat him from within, making him unreasonably suspicious. He turned his friends into enemies and imagined them plotting against him, while his inability to quit conquering caused his men—many of whom had families in Macedonia—despite their reverence for his military genius, to become disgruntled with their lot. Yet while in that rage were the seeds of his own destruction, it was the fuel for an unparalleled achievement. When Alexander died at the age of 32, he was undefeated king of over half the known world. Arguably no single person, left- or right-handed, has ever been as powerful.

# Julius Caesar

**100–44 BC**

IN 69 BC JULIUS CAESAR, SERVING AS A QUAESTOR (LIEUTENANT Governor) in Spain, was approaching his 31st birthday. In a moment of leisure he was reading a history of his great left-handed predecessor, Alexander the Great, when Caesar suddenly burst into tears. When his friends asked him what was wrong he replied, "Do you think I have not just cause to weep when I consider that Alexander at my age had conquered so many nations, and I have all this time done nothing that is memorable?"

By the time of his death, 25 years later, Julius Caesar was the greatest of Romans, a man who fought brilliantly with lefty cunning and honor against his military and political adversaries. His name "Caesar" would later mutate to become *czar* in Russian and *kaiser* in German. The most formidable conqueror since Alexander the Great, he would be remembered for the phrase *veni, vidi, vici* ("I came, I saw, I conquered"). His conquest of Gaul resulted in 800 conquered cities, 300 subdued tribes, 1 million men sold into slavery and another 1 million dead in the battlefields. Gaul would remain loyal to Rome until the fall of the Western Empire 500 years later. Julius Caesar's political legacy was also considerable and included the consolidation of the Roman Empire and improving the lot of the poor. After little more than a year of full power, he was assassinated, and it is interesting to wonder what he might have achieved if he had survived.

While he was weeping in Spain, however, his reputation was that of a profligate youth gifted with a silver tongue to match the silver spoon of his aristocratic birth. Alexander was a spur to his ambitious and ruthless mind. By the time Caesar's life was over he would have displayed much of the left-handed valor of his hero, and the world would know that the two of them had much in common, not least the lefty advantage of being able to outwit their opponents on the battlefield with unorthodox methods.

## CONQUERING THE PIRATES

**CONQUERING THE PIRATES** Although he didn't take an army into battle until relatively late in life, from an early age Caesar displayed the combination of tactical brilliance and unconventionality which are the hallmarks of the left-handed conqueror. The first major instance of this on record was when he set off for Rhodes in 75 BC to study oratory and was captured by pirates.

Most people when captured tend to be overwhelmed by their fear. They obey the power dynamics and become compliant toward the people who are holding the swords over their heads. The pirates were Cicilians, renowned in their time for being among the most bloodthirsty people in the world, as likely to kill someone as soon as look at them. All the more reason then to hope for their mercy. Not Caesar. Rather than huddle and hope, he attacked from a position of utmost weakness using strategies learned in his study of oratory. When the pirates demanded a ransom of 20 talents, he ridiculed them, offering to give them 50 instead because the pirates had failed to understand his status. Having sent most of his fellow travelers away to raise the ransom, he was left alone with the pirates. Yet instead of capitulating to their demands, he continued to disrespect them spectacularly.

When he wanted to sleep, he ordered them to make no noise. He wrote poems and speeches which he delivered to his piratical audience. If they didn't appreciate them, he called them illiterate and barbarous to their faces. He threatened to execute them. This went on for 38 whole days. Rather than kill him for his insolence (they were wealthy enough not to need the 50 talents) the pirates were captivated by Caesar's brave display and attributed his trash talking to simplicity and boyish playfulness. Not only was this brave, it was also classic left-handed thinking, the kind which uses reverse psychology to throw the enemy off balance. Caesar could have waited passively to be ransomed. Instead, with trust in his intuitions, he bravely abused his captors, despite their reputation for ruthlessness and violence. This unconventional approach had the unlikely consequence of Caesar earning his captors' almost affectionate respect. He had subverted the natural order of his predicament.

When his ransom was paid and the pirates released him, Caesar went straight to the port of Miletus where he took command of a number of ships and went back and surprised the pirates at the island where they had been holding him hostage. His small force captured most of them and he also secured their treasure, most of which he gave to Junius, Governor of Asia, in exchange for the right to determine the fate of the pirates. Having established a semi-friendly bond with Caesar, the pirates were surprised to hear him give the order for their crucifixion.

PREVIOUS PAGE: BUST OF JULIUS CAESAR. THE ROMANS WERE KEEN ON THE "VERISTIC," OR REALISTIC PORTRAIT, RATHER THAN THE IDEALIZED GREEK FORM.

## UNDERDOG SMARTS

**UNDERDOG SMARTS** A notable tendency in lefties is that because they have been a suppressed minority, they often ally themselves with the underdog. In Caesar's day, the main political division in Rome was between those who conservatively advocated the continued rights of the aristocracy and the populists who courted the support of the everyday people. Although of aristocratic birth, Caesar established his political power base by gaining popularity with his soldiers and the plebeians (commoners) of Rome.

Winning over the people was largely a matter of "bread and circuses." Caesar became known for his largesse. As Plutarch observed:

> He was unsparing in his outlays of money, and was thought to be purchasing a transient and short-lived fame at a great price, though in reality he was buying things of the highest value at a small price. We are told, accordingly, that before he entered upon any public office he was thirteen hundred talents in debt. Again, being appointed curator of the Appian Way, he expended upon it vast sums of his own money; and again, during his aedileship, he furnished three hundred and twenty pairs of gladiators, and by lavish provision besides for theatrical performances, processions, and public banquets, he washed away all memory of the ambitious efforts of his predecessors in the office. By these means he put the people in such a humour that every man of them was seeking out new offices and new honours with which to requite him.

Caesar's actions went against the grain since most Roman politicians' idea of office was to cement their own financial gain. While being laughed at by many in his own class for his profligacy, he managed to earn the support of the people, something which would protect him against his political enemies. Again, Caesar showed that lefty capability for achieving one's goals by turning the established way of doing things on its head.

Caesar's counter-intuitive lefty thinking is also evidenced by Dio Cassius's observation that, "He showed himself perfectly prepared to serve and flatter everybody, even ordinary people . . . and he did not mind temporarily groveling." Again we are confronted with a man whose natural stigma as a lefty, combined with his aristocratic pedigree, provided him with the ability to understand and operate easily within the full social spectrum. Lefty thinking ensured that Caesar wasn't captive to his pride or social position and, as a consequence, his ambition had full rein to operate in the most strategically advantageous manner. His skills in oratory were paralleled by his skills as an actor. Throughout his life Caesar would be able to transform his personality to meet the demands of a given situation while never losing sight of his own goals.

**GALLING THE GAULS** One of Caesar's great strengths as a military commander was his ability to inspire the loyalty of his men. This loyalty was partly based on his populist sensibility and his reputation for generosity in sharing the spoils of victory with his army. Yet, it was also because he had sufficient empathy with his men to understand what they wanted from their leader. It was a form of charisma he shared with

## LEFTY LINKS

1. Alexander the Great was a powerful source of inspiration and emulation for the young Caesar. Caesar chastised himself for having achieved nothing by the age of 31, by which time Alexander had conquered most of the known world. It would be another 10 years before Caesar would lead his first military campaign, at which age Alexander had been dead for almost a decade.

2. Caesar was not the only left-handed Roman emperor, although he was by far the greatest. Other lefty emperors included the talented and troubled Tiberius (42 BC–37 AD) who ended his life in paranoid, decadent isolation on the isle of Capris, and Commodius (161–192), who is widely considered one of the worst Roman emperors of all. He believed he was the reincarnation of Hercules, and used to fight as a gladiator, where he would arm the disabled with sponges then put them to the sword. A psychopath and hedonist, he was running the empire into the ground until he was murdered in his bath by a wrestler called Narcissus. Both Tiberius and Commodius were afflicted by the left-hander's increased disposition toward mental illness.

Alexander and Napoleon, whose soldiers also out-performed other armies through their loyalty to their commander.

Despite being an epileptic and having the soft white skin of the pampered classes, Caesar amazed his troops with his powers of endurance. In the first Gallic War against the Helvetii, in what is today known as Switzerland, after some initial victories Caesar was surprised by his enemies and forced to retreat to a place of defensible refuge. At this stage, he was presented with a horse, presumably as a means of making a prudent escape. But Caesar preferred to remain with his troops. Even more exceptional was that, once he had made the decision to fight, he refused to use the horse. He earned the awe and loyalty of his men by arguing that the horse was better left for pursuing the enemy after the battle had been won. He then marched off on foot at the head of his army to confront the enemy. The whole campaign could have turned at that point, yet Caesar's ability to look from the outside in and force his will upon the action was crucial. The ensuing battle lasted from morning till midnight with the Romans eventually triumphing. Through his unconventional entirely intuitive action, Caesar turned his army into a powerfully coherent force.

Although Caesar showed a complete lack of mercy to the pirates who had captured him but treated him well, his attitude toward the Gauls, once he had vanquished them, was entirely different. The Gauls had razed much of their own land and cities with the intention of denying Caesar's army supplies. Yet once he had defeated them, instead of slaughtering or selling them into slavery, he made them resettle their own land under the banner of Rome. This clever strategy showed great flexibility and foresight, and none of the bloodlust for revenge, which often erupts in the aftermath of such fiercely fought battles. It ensured a vacuum wasn't created that would entice the Germans over the Rhine to try and colonize Gaul, while giving the Romans a buffer zone against other yet-to-be conquered Gauls. Just as importantly, it gave Caesar a power base from which to continue his conquests, safe from, but still reasonably close to the political whirligig of Rome.

**DEFEATING POMPEY** Caesar displayed many of the identifiable qualities of the left-handed conqueror and he therefore had the ability to surprise his enemy with left-handed thought. In the Roman army at the time, soldiers were taught the difference between left and right by their correspondence with the hands holding shield and sword respectively, and orders to change direction were often given using these words. With such regimentation and the technological constraints of the day, the movement of armies was slower and more conventional than today. Having a talented and charismatic commander was an asset, even more so if he was left-handed. Forced to translate the right-handed organization of the army into his left-handed mind, the left-handed commander was more capable of

OPPOSITE: A STATUE OF JULIUS CAESAR DRESSED IN ARMOR, C.50 BC.

## THE RIGHT-HANDED SHAKE

When people put out their right hands to shake when greeting, they are following a custom established by Julius Caesar. The handshake originated as a guarded method for establishing trust between strangers. By taking hold of each other's hands, the shakers are ensuring that they aren't going to be punched or stabbed. But why would a left-handed Roman emperor enshrine the right-handed handshake as the primary way for men to greet each other? Easy. Because it keeps the left hand free to attack while the right-hander's strong arm is too busy being polite. Unfortunately, it was no use in preventing Caesar from eventually being stabbed in the back.

arriving at novel military strategies which had the dual advantage of inspiring his own men and vanquishing the enemy through the power of sheer surprise.

Caesar's first taste of true power came as a consequence of his victories in Gaul when he became part of the First Triumvirate with Crassus, the richest man in Rome and the celebrated General Pompey. It was an alliance cleverly put together by Caesar. His attempts to win popularity with the people had put him into debt which Crassus was able to help him out of, while Caesar surprised his political enemies by concluding an alliance with Pompey and sealing it with the successful marriage of his daughter, Julia, to the older general. But when Crassus was killed in an ill-advised military campaign against the Parthians and Julia died in childbirth, the alliance dissolved and it wasn't long before Pompey and Caesar were at war in the struggle for control of Rome.

The civil war was a protracted one, fought throughout the Roman Empire. Battles were waged in Gaul, Africa, Greece and Italy itself between two leaders with exemplary military records. The crucial moment came in Greece in 48 BC. Caesar had followed Pompey's army across the Adriatic, but was outnumbered by more than three to one. The two enemies ended up camped either side of a stream near a place called Dyrrhachium, where they attempted to deprive each other of supplies. Caesar mounted a siege and built a fortified wall 17 miles long around Pompey's army and also succeeded in blocking his supply of fresh water. Pompey's army was unable to breach the wall until two of Caesar's soldiers, who had been caught stealing, managed to escape to Pompey's camp where they informed him of the weakest point. Pompey's army breached the wall and set up a camp outside it, from which they were able to attack Caesar's smaller army. Caesar was forced to retreat. Yet having enforced the retreat, Pompey hesitated in prosecuting the advantage. The moment was lost and Caesar was able to resupply his army. Caesar stated, "Today the victory had been the enemy's had there been any one among them to gain it." Put another way, if Caesar had been in charge of Pompey's army, the Civil War would have been over.

The subsequent battle of Pharsalus in August 48 BC effectively ended the civil war and demonstrated Caesar's clear strategical superiority to his vacillating enemy. Caesar was again outnumbered, yet after several days of jockeying for position, he taunted Pompey so brilliantly that pride forced Pompey to take up a position on level ground. Pompey's army was arranged with his right wing protected by the river. In the center were Syrian and African troops. Pompey gambled by stacking his left flank with his entire cavalry, archers and slingers as well as a legion of infantry. Outnumbering Caesar's cavalry seven to one, Pompey was confident of outflanking Caesar's right and winning the war with minimal loss of life.

Caesar, however, saw this as a chance to counter Pompey's one-dimensional plan. He thinned his infantry out to match the length of

Pompey's numerically superior lines at considerably less depth. His infantry were ordered to hold firm and were not expected to break through the enemy's ranks. He put his much smaller cavalry on the right to counter Pompey's cavalry. The relative numerical weakness was a huge risk, yet Caesar gambled that Pompey would focus his attack at this point precisely because of this. He further reduced his main infantry lines by removing 3,000 of his best men, who he put in a semi-concealed position behind his cavalry and right flank infantry.

Caesar, and not Pompey, ordered the initial advance and the battle began slowly as a series of infantry skirmishes until Pompey finally unleashed his cavalry. His horsemen hit Caesar's cavalry hard, and almost broke through. Pompey ordered his archers and slingers, who were behind the cavalry, to assist in the assault with heavy blanket covering fire. At this point Pompey must have felt his success was almost assured. Yet, just as Caesar's cavalry were beginning to retreat, he ordered his reserve infantry to launch their surprise assault. Using their javelin-like pila, Caesar's 3,000 infantry attacked the 7,000 Pompeian cavalry with direct orders from Caesar to aim for the faces of the riders. Why? Caesar had noticed the men in this unit were young, particularly good looking and vain, and would therefore value their faces. Caesar's plan was a resounding success and the cavalry was routed. As Pompey's cavalry fled, they exposed the archers and slingers. Caesar then turned to attack Pompey's exposed left flank, which crumbled. Pompey panicked. Although he still had a strong numerical superiority, he had no back-up plan. Unlike Caesar in Gaul, he retreated to his camp while his army was decimated. When defeat became clear, instead of committing suicide as an honorable Roman was supposed to do, he abandoned his army to the enemy and fled. The civil war was effectively over.

The battle of Pharsalus was fundamentally a war of left versus right. The right-handed Pompey relied on conventional logic and numerical superiority. Caesar, on the other hand, used the left-handed qualities of surprise and intuition, by holding his infantry back and intuitively adopting the unorthodox tactic of attacking the enemy cavalry's faces rather than their horses, to cause panic.

As a left-hander forced from birth to interpret a world that doesn't fit, Caesar had that crucial extra degree of thinking, giving him the ability to intuit Pompey's tactics and come up with his own novel and successful strategy. The importance to history of this left-handed moment cannot be underestimated. This victory of Caesar set up a system of inherited imperial power which would help make the Roman Empire the undisputed leading power in the Ancient World.

## CAESAR'S LEFTY TRAITS

**INTUITIVE** Caesar's behavior in situations such as his kidnapping by the pirates illustrates how he was capable of using his instincts to get out of a jam.

**EMPATHETIC** Like Alexander the Great and Napoleon, Caesar was able to put himself in the shoes of his soldiers which, combined with his bravery, earned him fearsome loyalty.

**VISUAL-SPATIAL ABILITY** In Caesar's defeat of Pompey he displayed the ability common to all great military commanders to visualize a battlefield, anticipate the enemy's strategy and then devise a plan to outwit them.

**LATERAL THINKING** Very few generals would have thought of using the vanity of his enemies against them, and conceive a novel mode of attack to rout a numerically superior army.

**EXPERIMENTAL** Caesar was prepared to gamble with new tactics on the battlefield and always tried to fit his strategy to a specific context.

# Joan of Arc

THERE ARE FEW MORE ASTONISHING FIGURES IN HISTORY THAN THE late-medieval, cross-dressing, virginal, lefty saint and French military commander, Joan of Arc. She was born a simple peasant girl in a period when France was in thrall to the Hundred Years War. Guided by divine voices Joan surmounted almost impossible societal hurdles, in a world riven by class and chivalric codes, to lead her army to a series of important victories which changed the balance of the war. She was captured in battle, sold to the English, convicted of heresy in a medieval show-trial and eventually burned at the stake. She was only 19 years old. Not long after her death, when the Dauphin Charles she had fought for became legitimate King of France, she was rehabilitated by the church in a reverse trial. The reversal was taken to the extreme in 1920 when the Catholic Church made her a saint.

**HEARING VOICES** As a child, Joan was remembered by her fellow villagers for being helpful, friendly and devout. When she was 12 years old, she said she was visited by the Archangel Michael, the protective angel of France, who told her that her fate was to lay siege to the town of Orleans and, by doing so, help the Armagnac claimant to the throne, the Dauphin Charles, to become King of France. The Armagnac faction, with whom Joan was allied, was at war with the Burgundians, who were also French but allied with the British. Known as the Hundred Years War, skirmishes and battles between these forces took place across the countryside. Towns and farms were often pillaged by poorly supplied troops from both sides of the battle.

The Archangel Michael told Joan to listen and follow the advice of St. Catherine and St. Margaret, virgin martyrs who were popular in the Middle Ages. These days if someone goes about telling people they have heard the voice of an angel, they are usually diagnosed with

## LEFTY LINKS

1. It's easy to underestimate how complete the Christian worldview actually was in medieval Europe. Christian symbolism almost unfailingly viewed the left as evil, secondary or inferior. The devil, for instance, was depicted with his left hand outstretched, while passages from the Bible, such as the following from Matthew 25, show a clear preference for the right: "Then shall the king say unto them on his right hand, come ye blessed of my father, inherit the kingdom prepared for you. . . . Then shall He say also unto them on the left hand, depart from me ye cursed into everlasting fire. Prepare for the devil and his angels."

As Rowena and Rupert Shepherd point out in *1000 Symbols*, in Christianity "the right side of the body represents the first stage of Creation, daytime, consciousness, Adam, Man and active power. The left represents the second stage of Creation, Earth, matter, Eve, Women and receptivity." Left-handed people were treated with considerable suspicion in the Middle Ages, and were more vulnerable to being charged with ecclesiastical crimes, such as heresy and witchcraft, which were often trumped up—as in the case of Joan's trial—to preserve the interests of those in control of the status quo. If you were in the wrong place at the wrong time, merely being left-handed made you more prone to being burned at the stake for being either a heretic or a witch.

2. It is interesting to note here that left-handers are more prone to schizophrenia than their right-handed counterparts. This is perhaps the downside of the heightened powers of sensitivity and empathy left-handers often exhibit. Some research has shown that left-handers tend to have greater schizoid tendencies than right-handers and furthermore, those with schizoid tendencies that don't deteriorate into schizophrenia tend often to be better lateral thinkers than those without Some of the more conspicuous schizoid personalities among the lefties in these pages include Lewis Carroll, Nietzsche and Jimi Hendrix.

3. One of Joan's biggest fans was fellow lefty Mark Twain.

schizophrenia, treated with drugs or worse, and shunted to the margins of society. In fact, being a left-hander, Joan was actually statistically more vulnerable to schizophrenia. However, in the Middle Ages, prophets and visionaries who claimed to be in contact with God were fairly common, and there was certainly not the same stigma attached to the idea of paranormal experience as there is today. Unlike most contemporary schizophrenics, Joan was very fond of her voices and claimed they brought her warmth and joy. With the exception of some moments before her execution, Joan felt herself to be in the permanent presence of the divine and it was this certainty that enabled her to act with the kind of total conviction necessary to bring others into her orbit and achieve her goals. The voices accompanied Joan throughout her adolescence. They advised her to maintain her virginity in order that she would be able to serve a higher purpose. In her seventeenth year, this higher purpose was revealed when she was told that her role would be to assist the Dauphin Charles to be crowned King of France.

An amazing aspect of Joan's personality was her ability to persuade men in positions of authority to adopt her cause. The first person she had to convince of her mission was her local lord, Robert de Baudricourt. As an illiterate peasant girl of 17, it was surprising that he even deigned to see her when she turned up in her traditional red peasant's dress with the request to raise an army. De Baudricourt was a notorious philanderer and people were also surprised that Joan escaped with her virginity intact, especially since it is on record that she had very attractive breasts.

Joan's manner of approach threw de Baudricourt off guard. Without granting the deference she was supposed to pay to his social position, she introduced herself by saying:

> I have come from my Lord so that you may tell the Dauphin to be brave and and keep going in his war against his enemies. Before mid Lent the Lord will help him. My Lord who the kingdom actually belongs to, wants the Dauphin to be King and to rule this kingdom. The Dauphin will be made king despite his enemies, and I have been chosen to take him to the coronation.

## WINNING OVER THE KING

If Joan's success in winning over de Baudricourt was a major coup, her achievement in winning over the eventual King of France was nothing short of phenomenal. By all accounts Charles was a fairly unspectacular candidate to benefit from the religio-political miracle Joan was selling. He was weak-chinned, squinty-eyed and stumpy-legged with a reputation for vacillation and over-dependence upon those who surrounded him. When Joan arrived, the Dauphin and his advisors were initially reluctant to meet her. She was forced to wait for more than two days outside the castle at Chinon before they let the drawbridge down. Once they did, they set a test for her. Gathering

300 elaborately dressed courtiers, they demanded that Joan look through them and select the King. Using her lefty intuition, she was able to look beyond the false symbolic hierarchy of appearance and spot the moderately dressed Charles as the genuine article.

Once she had achieved this feat, Joan was granted an audience with Charles. What she then accomplished was amazing: she persuaded Charles to give her the Kingdom of France. The deed was witnessed by four of the King's secretaries. Soon after she gave the Kingdom to God. Then, having done this, she re-invested Charles with the Kingdom, acting under the authority of God. For an illiterate peasant girl with no schooling, this was brilliant and complicated stuff.

A final test saw Joan being examined by a learned bunch of ecclesiasts, including the Archbishop of Reims and the Royal Confessors, whose job it was to determine whether her mission was divinely inspired. As Joan would later discover, the line between divinity and heresy could be extremely subjective and she certainly wasn't the first person to be burned on falsified charges. The ecclesiasts decided Joan was the fulfilling of a prophecy that a virgin would save France. Joan was given a suit of armor, a sword and set off toward the enemy with a retinue of 4,000 men.

**JOAN WARRIOR VIRGIN** The argument that left-handers are made by having extra testosterone is backed up by Joan's cavalier behavior on the battlefield. Her fury and eagerness to fight were on display from the very beginning at the Battle of Orleans. The commander of the French forces was the Bastard of Orleans, aka Dunois, the illegitimate son of the Duke of Orleans who was a captive of the English. When Joan arrived in late April 1429, the English had laid siege to the city of 30,000 people for six months and the citizens' capacity to resist was beginning to fade. Joan arrived ready to attack, but the mistrust of some of the experienced military saw her sidelined as part of a plan to help supply the city through its one remaining accessible gate. They didn't tell Joan, however, of the secondary role they intended her to play and when she found out she went crazy, telling the bastard, who was at least half royal, that if anyone tried to con her like that again, she'd cut off their head. Dunois merely replied that he was sure she would.

The immense chutzpah of her dealings with her superiors was compounded by her bravery in the battle. After a series of successful skirmishes, in which Joan had a significant impact, the Battle of Orleans began in earnest on May 7, 1429. When the army charged, Joan was at the forefront. At noon, she was hit above the left breast by an arrow which buried itself six inches into her. She had already told her confessor this was something her voices had foretold. Joan pulled the arrow out herself and, after allowing her wound to be dressed with animal fat, she rested a while before rejoining the battle, which greatly boosted the morale of the French troops. At 8 pm, the horn for retreat was blown, but Joan ignored it. She was on foot, part of an

## MAID WITH TESTOSTERONE

Around the time she went to see de Baudricourt, Joan self-consciously adopted the nickname, La Pucelle, or the Maid. She did this both to emphasize her virginity and to deny her femininity. The closest women usually came to being in the army was as camp-following prostitutes. Joan also adopted the wearing of male clothes since it was harder to be sexually assaulted while wearing them, but also because it distinguished her from the other women and enhanced her capacity to be accepted as one of the boys.

Joan was without doubt a prototype tomboy, passionate, hot-headed, idealistic and rash. It has long been known that men are twice as likely to be left-handed as women. Some scientists have claimed that a cause of left-handedness is exposure to extra testosterone in the womb that favors the development of the right hemisphere of the brain. This might explain Joan's alpha male approach to life. It also casts light on a possible cause for the kind of testosterone-fueled rage found in many of the great left-handers in this book: Alexander, Caesar, Napoleon, John McEnroe and Michelangelo, to name but a few.

Joan was also renowned for her temper. When the powerful Duke Charles of Lorraine, hearing of Joan's powers, summoned her to cure him, she went and lectured him that she could do nothing for his health, but he should give up his mistress and go back to his wife. Surprised and chastened, the duke made her a gift of some money and a horse.

PAGE 45: JOAN OF ARC AT THE CORONATION OF THE DAUPHIN AS KING CHARLES VII IN REIMS CATHEDRAL, ACCOMPANIED BY HER SQUIRE, CHAPLAIN AND PAGES.

FOLLOWING PAGES: JOAN OF ARC ARRIVES AT CHINON CASTLE TO MEET THE DAUPHIN DURING THE HUNDRED YEARS WAR.

assault that involved crossing a moat and scaling the walls to the city. The soldier next to her, who was carrying her standard, collapsed with exhaustion and passed it on to a soldier who wasn't under Joan's command. When Joan saw this, she was enraged and rushed up through a torrent of stones that was being slung by the English, to take hold of the standard herself. All the other soldiers saw the standard blown by the wind so that it pointed in the direction of the enemy—an omen of victory. The troops headed back into battle and by the morning the English had decamped and, with victory hers to savor, Joan became known for the first time as the Maid of Orleans.

**DOWNFALL** With the English having retreated from the Loire Valley, Charles was crowned King of France in the cathedral city of Reims, just as Joan had predicted. In keeping with her impetuous character, she agitated for an immediate attack against the English and Burgundian forces that were holding Paris. She was probably right, yet Charles was vacillating and his chief advisor strongly favored a diplomatic end to the war. Charles signed a 15-day truce, which was merely a ploy for the enemy to bring in new troops and better organize their defense.

Joan's fortunes declined markedly in her second series of campaigns. After a number of unsuccessful skirmishes, her army was temporarily disbanded and Joan was stuck at court, whose ornate and stultifying manners clashed with her impatient spirit. Like Leonardo da Vinci, Joan was a person who preferred nature over culture and, like Alexander the Great, she treasured the glory of battle over the trappings of luxury.

When, in 1430, Charles finally decided a diplomatic solution was impossible, the army marched toward Paris. In the interim, however, the army had been underfed and underpaid and had lost much of its enthusiasm for the fight. After an all-night ride, Joan attempted to persuade her 300 men to take on 6,000 Burgundians at the town of Soissons. Drastically outnumbered, she made assault after assault until her men were too exhausted to fight any more. Those who could retreated, but Joan continued to fight until she was surrounded and knocked off her horse by a Picardy archer. She was then sold to the English, tried for heresy and burned at the stake and she was still only 19 years old.

Joan of Arc's success had been brief but phenomenal. She lacked the training of other great commanders, but not the courage. When Charles eventually took Paris in 1437, he organized for the rehabilitation of Joan's reputation and she remains one of the great enigmas of history, the left-handed peasant girl who came from nowhere, guided by angelic voices, to lead the French army into one of the greatest victories it had ever known. As Winston Churchill was later to remark in *The Birth of Britain*:

Joan was a being so uplifted from the ordinary run of mankind that she finds no equal in a thousand years.

## JOAN OF ARC'S LEFTY TRAITS

**INTUITIVE** Joan's whole life was based on gut instinct guided by divine voices and acted out with tremendous temerity.

**EMPATHETIC** Joan had the ability to see into people, especially important men, which made it possible for her to achieve her unlikely strategies.

**HOT-TEMPERED** Joan's rage in battle was astonishing, while she was almost as fierce with those who crossed her path. It was as if she was channeling the wrath of her God.

**ICONOCLASTIC** Joan was so iconoclastic that no other woman has yet been able to fully follow her example. Of all the people in this book, she is probably the most unique. Her iconoclasm also cost her her life as she was burned at the stake for heresy.

**SELF-TAUGHT** It's arguable that Joan even educated herself. A peasant girl with no formal schooling, she was able to outwit members of the nobility with pure instinct and the strength of her conviction in her guiding voices.

**FANTASIST** Joan harnessed her imagination and probable schizoid character to become one of the greatest figures in history.

OPPOSITE: BEFORE GOING IN TO BATTLE, JOAN OF ARC HAD HER STANDARD PAINTED WITH AN IMAGE OF CHRIST IN JUDGMENT AND A BANNER MADE BEARING THE NAME OF JESUS CHRIST.

# Leonardo da Vinci

1452–1519 WHO WOULD HAVE THOUGHT THAT THE GREATEST MIND IN WESTERN civilization would have been an illegitimate, gay, vegetarian lefty? No name in history is more synonymous with genius than Leonardo da Vinci, who was all of these things. In addition to creating the world's most famous painting, the *Mona Lisa*, Leonardo (as he is best known) had an unbounded natural curiosity. His notebooks contained ideas for inventions and techniques centuries ahead of his time, in fields as diverse as engineering, anatomy, aviation, aerodynamics, hydraulics, military technology and art. Of all the Italian "renaissance men," Leonardo was the most outstanding; a polymath whose vast talent traversed the boundaries of art and science like few others ever have.

While his homosexuality and illegitimacy gave Leonardo the freedom from the masculine conventions of career and family to pursue his creativity, his left-handedness had a crucial impact on his personality and productivity. In many ways, he was the quintessential left-hander, the outsider whose sheer brilliance, original thinking and enhanced visual-spatial skills took him to the center of his world. With his fellow artists Michelangelo and Raphael, Leonardo forms one of the most fascinating lefty clusters of history. Without these three, the Italian Renaissance, a crucial period in the development of Western civilization, would have been far less interesting.

**EARLY LEONARDO** Leonardo was born to an unmarried peasant girl called Caterina. His father, who recognized Leonardo as his son, but did not marry his mother, was Ser Piero da Vinci, a young lawyer who later became prominent in Florentine circles.

Leonardo's childhood was spent in the rustic environment of Vinci (his surname literally means "from Vinci") a small town outside of Florence, where his father's family had its country estates. Because he was illegitimate, Leonardo didn't receive much formal education. It wasn't until

## LEFTY LINKS

1. Leonardo's greatest connections with other lefty geniuses in history are undoubtedly with Michelangelo and Raphael, both of whom he knew. In their personalities, Leonardo and Michelangelo were chalk and cheese rivals, mainly because of the latter's paranoid competitiveness—though Leonardo was capable of being dismissive in his opinions of other artists. Raphael shared and extended upon Leonardo's reputation for urbanity and grace, but lacked his all-round genius.

2. Leonardo's intuitive genius for mechanical design is perhaps most noticeable in the equally self-taught brilliance of automobile pioneer Henry Ford, while his belief that nature operated according to mathematical laws was furthered by Isaac Newton.

3. Another characteristic Leonardo shared with Henry Ford was vegetarianism. An eccentric lifestyle choice for a fifteenth-century Florentine, it's a trait shared with other lefty greats including Paul McCartney and Mahatma Gandhi.

4. One of the most significant aspects of Leonardo's notebooks was the use of mirror writing. This is very rare in real life, but gets a famous fictional outing at the beginning of *Through the Looking Glass*, written by lefty fantasist Lewis Carroll.

using oil had begun with Flemish painters, such as Jan van Eyck, and was known to the Italian painters, but they generally used it only as a surface glaze. Leonardo was one of the first to use oils as his primary medium. The longer drying time helped him to achieve the level of detail he required and allowed him to create a stronger sense of depth by adding layers of paint. Throughout his life he was always open to new ways of doing things, and his willingness to depart from the known often delivered excellent results.

His creativity was liberated by his technical experiments with oils. His depictions of people and nature, honed by his anatomical investigations, were richly realistic. Looking at a Leonardo painting, you see how much accurate detail there is in the natural settings of their backgrounds. Leonardo was a perfectionist. In painting, for instance, he pioneered techniques, such as sfumato (fine shading), in which he applied a haze to objects in the background of the picture. This mimicked the effect of looking into the distance in Tuscany's distinctive light, and gave his work a sense of depth that other painters had not yet been able to achieve.

Leonardo had a strong dislike of people who bolstered their own views by quoting the experts who had gone before them. He believed they were the owners of second-hand knowledge when it was knowledge gained from direct experience that counted:

No one should ever imitate the style of another because he will be called a nephew and not a child of nature with regard to art.

This attitude is again typical "right-brain thinking." Eschewing the accepted wisdom that artists were beholden first and foremost to tradition, Leonardo championed originality, a quality which was both a marker of both genius and great art. But what is accepted wisdom now was radical then, which made him an iconoclast—another characteristic lefty trait.

According to one of his early biographers, Giorgio Vasari, Leonardo's talent was formidable from the outset. So good was the apprentice's work on one of Verrocchio's paintings that the latter apparently retired from painting when he saw it. But Leonardo's gift was coupled with a renowned tendency not to finish what he had started.

A typical example was the altarpiece Leonardo was commissioned to paint for the monks of S. Donato a Scopeto in Florence, the work which became known as *Adoration of the Magi*. Leonardo was expected to take around two years to complete it, with an agreed outside limit for the job of three years. As payment he would receive a stake in some land that had been bequeathed to the monks. The initial agreement was made in March 1481. In early 1482, much to the chagrin of the monks, Leonardo packed his bags and headed to Milan with the painting only partly finished. It was never delivered. He left what he had completed with a friend for safe-keeping and it eventually ended up in the Medici Collection as an unfinished work, and is now in the Uffizi Gallery. (The monks were forced to approach a lesser but more reliable artist, Filippino Lippi, to get their altarpiece; Lippi also saved the day for the Florentine government when Leonardo failed to deliver an altarpiece it had commissioned.) In Milan, Leonardo was commissioned to make a massive bronze sculpture of a horse in honor of Francesco Sforza. He got as far as making the clay model. However, he dallied at the point of casting the bronze, distracted by scientific experiments and a foray into directing pageants. He delayed so long that war broke out with the French, the metal was diverted for military purposes and the clay model was destroyed when the invading army used it for archers' target practice.

Right-handed thought tends to prefer a step-by-step process—completing one thing before beginning another. In contrast, left-handers are known for their divergent (rather than convergent) thought patterns. In some, this produces a superior capacity to multi-task. Leonardo, however, was a victim of his own incessant curiosity and perfectionism, as well as the often conflicting demands of his patrons. He would frequently become sidetracked by other ideas and projects. While painting a fresco, for instance, he would have a brainwave concerning a pet project, such as flight, and he would abandon the painting to pursue the new idea. His low completion rate demonstrates the risks of divergent thinking. It's unlikely that he completed more than 20 paintings in a 46-year career—in a way he had too much genius for one person to be able to effectively manage.

**THE NOTEBOOKS** The greatest insight into the way Leonardo thought can perhaps be gained from looking at his copious notebooks, which are full of sketches, inquiries and observations as well as jokes, shopping lists and accounts. In these books there are meditations on the many things that intrigued that mighty brain, including art, engineering, flying, architecture, philosophy and mathematics. Leonardo often had a notebook hanging from his belt and would stop in the street to sketch observations or note down ideas. Paper was expensive, so the pages were cluttered, filled to their corners with drawings and writing that revealed the man's eclectic brilliance.

Leonardo was prone to signing his notebooks *disscepolo para sperientia*, which can be translated to mean a disciple of either experience or experiment. It is an indicator that he had forsaken Christianity as the organizing principle of his life. His refusal to accept tradition for tradition's sake meant that he had traded in what he regarded as the abstract values of Christianity, in favor of the kinds of truth that can be observed with the eye. In this, he was a forerunner of the Age of Reason (or Enlightenment) with its belief in science and the power of the human mind to penetrate the mysteries of nature.

**LEFT WING** One of Leonardo's great obsessions was the idea of human flight. In the notebook now known as the *Codex Atlanticus* he wrote:

> A bird is a machine working according to mathematical laws. It lies within the power of man to reproduce this machine with all its motions, but not with as much power . . . Such a machine constructed by man lacks only the spirit of the bird, and this spirit must be counterfeited by the spirit of man.

The possibility of flying occupied large periods of Leonardo's time. As a lefty, he was fascinated by flying because of the seeming impossibility of achieving it. To fly would surmount the ultimate frontier. The man who flew would no longer be subject to the conventions of his society on earth.

Leonardo's flying designs included a pyramid-shaped parachute, which was built in 2000, then tested from 10,000 feet by English skydiver Adrian Nicholas. It worked. He also designed a vertical flying machine that anticipated the helicopter, but his most notable flying machine was the *ucello*, or "great bird." For this, Leonardo put his amazing observational, anatomical and drawing skills to work figuring out how birds actually flew, then attempted to adapt his findings into the design of a machine that would allow humans to fly. Here again he was assisted by his left-handedness—left-handers are forced to adapt to a world of right-handed utensils from an early age. Their lives are marked by improvization in order to find a way of dealing with a world that never quite fits.

## LEONARDO'S LEFTY TRAITS

**VISUAL-SPATIAL SKILLS** In his painting, anatomical drawings, sketches and designs, Leonardo exhibited some of the best hand-eye skills of anyone in history, which he then turned into a practical philosophy that exemplified his belief in the superiority of observable or empirical knowledge.

**LATERAL THINKING** One of the great lateral thinkers, Leonardo came up with designs for machines such as submarines, helicopters and armored tanks hundreds of years before they were technologically possible.

**ICONOCLASTIC** Leonardo helped revolutionize the techniques of Italian painting, believed in the possibility of human flight and was a forerunner of the Age of Reason. He was also a vegetarian for ethical reasons, which made him very much a rarity in his society.

**SELF-TAUGHT** Leonardo lacked formal schooling and replaced it with self-education, based not on books but on the evidence nature presented to his powerful eye.

**EXPERIMENTAL** Leonardo often tested his inventions and was even rumored to have built a prototype airplane, which he attempted to fly (unsuccessfully) from the top of a hill outside Florence.

OPPOSITE: PEN AND INK DRAWING, *VITRUVIAN MAN*, SHOWING THE PROPORTIONS OF THE HUMAN FIGURE, C.1492.

PAGES 58–59: ALL TOGETHER, LEONARDO'S NOTEBOOKS CONTAIN AROUND 13,000 PAGES OF SKETCHES AND NOTES ON ART, SCIENCE AND PHILOSOPHY.

# Michelangelo

1475–1564

ALTHOUGH LEONARDO DA VINCI IS THE ARCHETYPAL LEFTY GENIUS, HE WAS not the only left-hander to dominate the art world of the Italian Renaissance. Michelangelo Buonarotti was born in 1475 when Leonardo was already 23 years old. By the time he died in 1564, at almost 90 years of age, Michelangelo was widely considered the great artistic genius of the Italian Renaissance, a brilliant sculptor, painter, architect and poet whose works, such as the ceiling of the Sistine Chapel, were unparalleled in their scale and achievement.

Michelangelo and Leonardo were conspicuous rivals. While they were both lefties, and possessed typical lefty talents—most obviously the enhanced visual-spatial skills often found in people with right-brain dominance—their personalities were very different. Leonardo was a self-educated polymath released from the burden of questing for social distinction by virtue of his illegitimacy. For Michelangelo the situation was rather different. To begin with he was the legitimate son of a family with claims to Tuscany's minor nobility. As such, Michelangelo was expected to follow his father, who was a magistrate, and seek employment that would be appropriate for the family's sense of social standing. However, Michelangelo had other ideas. As with Leonardo, his lefty genius for the visual arts was insuppressible.

**AN INNATE ARTIST** If Michelangelo's family were minor gentry, they were the impoverished kind and, with an increasing number of children, his father planned to apprentice his sons into relatively lucrative careers in the silk and wool guilds. To facilitate this, Michelangelo was placed in a school to learn the skills essential to becoming a merchant, such as grammar and math. However, he spent most of his time sketching, so much so that his father used to beat him for it. However, Michelangelo was stubborn. He became friendly with Francesco Granacci, who was apprenticed to the master painter Domenico Ghirlandajo. Granacci used to supply Michelangelo with copies of sketches and materials for the young artist to

work with. At the time, being an artist was a disreputable occupation for someone of noble birth and Michelangelo's father was appalled to see his son's strong predilection for an activity beneath his station. However, seeing the writing on the wall, he eventually capitulated to his son's wish to be allowed to express his enormous talent. At the age of 14, Michelangelo entered the studio of Ghirlandajo. Ironically, it turned out to be the best financial move the Buonarotti family ever made. While a brilliant artist, Michelangelo also proved himself, unlike Leonardo, to be an astute businessman and, throughout his long career, he bought a significant amount of property which added greatly to the family's prosperity and prestige.

**AN ANGRY ARTIST** The family resistance to Michelangelo's artistic aspirations had a definite effect on his psyche. Whereas Leonardo was known as a genial man, prone to procrastination and getting sidetracked, Michelangelo soon developed a reputation for a terrifying, obsessive perfectionism. His temper was legendary and he was unable to restrain his ire whether it was directed at a servant or a pope. The Florentines referred to his *terribilitas*, meaning "fearsome willpower." During his professional life, Michelangelo managed to escape getting into serious trouble for his temper by his awe-inspiring work and a personal devoutness, which he acquired from becoming a disciple of the fear-inducing fire and brimstone preacher Savonarola. In some ways, Michelangelo's temper resembled the existential fury that drove Alexander the Great. Both were men whose personalities were driven by the attempt to resolve powerful internal tension. Like the conqueror, Michelangelo's life was also played out in a competitive frenzy from which there was never any real chance of release.

**TRADING LEFTS** Michelangelo's relationships with other artists were notoriously thorny. Perhaps his most difficult relationship was with his fellow lefty Leonardo, whose genius Michelangelo felt he had to surmount in order to consolidate the recognition of his own. In many ways, he defined himself in opposition to Leonardo, a classic case of what the critic Harold Bloom has called the anxiety of influence, a kind of Oedipus complex of artistic inheritance. There's a case to be made that Michelangelo defined himself as an artist directly in opposition to Leonardo. Where Leonardo preferred painting, Michelangelo claimed sculpture to be the superior art form. Leonardo was noted for his commitment to nature, while Michelangelo viewed nature as an enemy that both art and culture had to overcome.

Following his painting apprenticeship, Michelangelo was effectively adopted into the humanities-saturated household of Florence's great ruler, Lorenzo "The Magnificent" de Medici, where he was taught the mystic rationalism of Neo-platonism. As a consequence, Michelangelo's art saw a return to classicism, a terrain that the self-educated Leonardo seldom chose for his subject matter. The differences were personal too.

OPPOSITE: PORTRAIT OF MICHELANGELO. THE ARTIST WAS SO FAMOUS THAT HE WAS THE FIRST WESTERN ARTIST WHO HAD A BIOGRAPHY PUBLISHED WHILE HE WAS STILL LIVING.

PAGE 63: MICHELANGELO'S *DAVID* ILLUSTRATES THE IDEA OF "DISEGNO," WHERE THE ARTIST'S INITIAL DESIGN OR "CONCEPT" IS ALL-IMPORTANT.

## MICHELANGELO'S LEFTY TRAITS

**VISUAL-SPATIAL ABILITY** Imagine standing in front of a block of marble and being able to hold an image in your head of how to achieve an almost perfect representation of the human form over thousands of hits with a chisel and hammer.

**HOT-TEMPERED** Michelangelo was one of the most famously grouchy artists of all time. Not even the Pope was immune from his rage. Most of all, however, it was directed inwardly.

**SOLITARY** Michelangelo's slovenly, disheveled appearance was positively anti-social, especially for an Italian. A severe predilection for secrecy and paranoia compounded this. The tension between his devoutness and his homosexuality didn't help either. He never married, and his one great love was Tomasso dei Cavalieri, a 23-year-old youth who Michelangelo met when he was 54.

**ICONOCLASTIC** Michelangelo's work in the Sistine Chapel saw the fusion of classical and biblical imagery. Michelangelo's painting of naked figures was viewed by some people as sacrilegious. Although he was perhaps unaware of it, Michelangelo was iconoclastic in that his art was central to the way the Renaissance increased the importance of the human at the expense of the divine.

**SELF-TAUGHT** Michelangeo was apprenticed to an artist and studied under the Medicis, where he absorbed the lessons of the classics. However, when Michelangelo was commissioned to paint the ceiling of the Sistine Chapel he had to teach himself the art of painting frescoes.

OPPOSITE: THE DOME OF ST. PETER'S BASILICA IN ROME, DESIGNED BY MICHELANGELO.

According to Paolo Giovio, a contemporary biographer writing around 1527, the two were chalk and cheese: Leonardo was elegant, Michelangelo slovenly; Leonardo well-mannered, Michelangelo anti-social; Leonardo famous for his generosity and grace, Michelangelo for his obsessive secrecy and terrible temper. Michelangelo also finished his commissions, something Leonardo often failed to do.

These two great left-handed artists probably didn't meet that frequently, but the sparks flew on at least one occasion when they did. Leonardo was walking by the seats at the Palazzo Spini, where a number of men were debating a passage in Dante's *Divine Comedy*. They called out to Leonardo hoping to ask him for his interpretation. At the same time, Michelangelo was approaching from another direction. Seeing him, Leonardo congenially told the gathering that Michelangelo would be able to explain it to them. Michelangelo, prone to paranoia, assumed Leonardo was mocking him and exploded, "Explain it yourself, you who have made the design of a horse to be cast in bronze but was unable to and abandoned it in shame." With this snarling reference to Leonardo's unfinished sculpture of the *Sforza Horse*, Michelangelo turned his back on the group and left, leaving the genial Leonardo red in the face. On the positive side, this tension between these egotistical and brilliant left-handers was at least partly responsible for generating some of the greatest art the world has ever seen.

**MAKING DAVID** If Michelangelo was openly contemptuous, Leonardo was privately dismissive of Michelangelo and his sculpture *David*. Although at times he worked in this medium, Leonardo was disdainful of sculpture per se. In his notebooks Leonardo wrote:

> The sculptor in creating his work does so by the strength of his arm by which he consumes the marble, or other obdurate material in which his subject is enclosed: and this is done by most mechanical exercise, often accompanied by great sweat which mixes with the marble dust and forms a kind of mud daubed all over his face. The marble dust flours him all over so that he looks like a baker; his back is covered with a snowstorm of chips, and his house is made filthy by the flakes and dust of stone.

It's easy to see how the elegant Leonardo might have found all this sweat and mess ungainly. Sculpture, however, was in sync with Michelangelo's temperament for several reasons. For one, the sheer physicality of it suited his angry temperament. Sculpting shapes out of marble blocks is ultimately a matter of creating beauty using controlled violence. The chisel has to be hammered into the stone thousands of times and, at each blow, there is the risk of making a mistake that cannot be undone.

Michelangelo's masterpiece, *David*, illustrates the immense effort that went into his work. The achievement of a man with remarkable willpower,

1. Michelangelo's paranoia and secrecy resemble that of left-handed scientist Isaac Newton. Both were solitary, hyper-competitive and hyper-sensitive to criticism. Both men held grudges, imagined rivals and magnified the antipathy of the rivals they actually had.

2. Being hyper-competitive is a personality trait often found in high achievers. The happiest people, however, seem to be those who achieve on their own terms, such as Leonardo. Many of the lefties in these pages were fiercely competitive. We can see this, for instance, in Nietzsche's attitude to his critics, or the angry antics of left-handed tennis players such as McEnroe and Navratilova, or in the lives of Alexander and Napoleon. It's even discernible in the guitar ambitions of Jimi Hendrix. Or take a look at the ruthless tactics of Microsoft under Bill Gates. While competitive relativity may be an aspect of many higher achievers keen to distinguish themselves from the herd, for the left-hander it's a little different, since they don't fully belong to the herd to begin with. In a sense, they are forced to compare themselves with the right-handed majority from the very beginning—which may explain, to some extent, why left-handers are more likely to be found at the upper and lower extremes of success.

3. A 2000 study by Canadian researchers found that homosexual men and women are more likely to be left-handed than their heterosexual counterparts. The reasons for this are unclear. However, it is possible that people who are different from the rest of the world are more likely to develop *more* differently as they reach maturity. The people surveyed in this book would tend to anecdotally support this theory. Michelangelo and Leonardo da Vinci were primarily homosexual, Alexander the Great was also known to sleep with men, computer scientist and code-breaker Alan Turing was gay, as is tennis star Martina Navratilova. Julius Caesar was also rumored to have enjoyed homosexual affairs. That's way above the 10 percent proportion of the population usually considered to be gay.

it took four years to carve the world's most famous sculpture. *David* was carved from a block of Carrara marble nicknamed "the Giant," which had been lying unused for 25 years after its serious flaws had defeated the talents of two eminent Florentine sculptors—Agostino di Duccio and Antonio Rossellino. Using the Giant was an act of sculptural one-upmanship and, in doing so, Michelangelo conquered both the marble and his predecessors' reputations.

*David* was based on the artistic principle of *disegno*, in which the success of an artwork consists in its correspondence to the artist's original conception. Within this idea, it was believed that sculpture was the finest form of art because its three-dimensionality most closely mimicked the divine creation. To make a sculpture of the male body was the ultimate artistic challenge, since it corresponded to what Renaissance people believed was God's highest creative act. Because sculpture is three-dimensional, it utilizes the superior visual and spatial abilities often associated with left-handedness even more than painting. Viewed from this perspective, Michelangelo's lefty genius is quite astonishing. When two anatomy professors from the University of Florence carried out the first anatomical survey of the statue during its cleaning in 2004, they found that, although *David* was not very well-endowed, the only physiological mistake Michelangelo had made was that there was a hollow instead of a muscle on the right side of the back, an error that the artist had acknowledged in correspondence of the time, where he said he hadn't had enough material to make the muscle.

Whereas Leonardo wanted to fly, at least part of Michelangelo had the dream of transcending his limitations and approaching God's capability by creating perfect artworks. There's more than a tinge of heresy in the immensity of Michelangelo's ambition. His ambition clashed with his devoutness (Michelangelo was no stranger to self-loathing) and this helped to generate the creative tension that kept him furiously brilliant for most of his life. As with Ancient World left-handed conquerors such as Alexander and Caesar, Michelangelo's kind of hyper-competitive over-reaching was insatiable, the product of an almost diabolical will. It can partly be attributed to the left-hander's insatiable desire to transform a world in which they never fully fit.

**PAINTING THE SISTINE CHAPEL** The ceiling of the Sistine Chapel was very much the product of Michelangelo's outrageous will. Although he had a distinct preference for sculpture, he was unable to resist Pope Julius II's entreaties to paint a fresco on the ceiling of the Chapel. Rumor has it that the idea of Michelangelo painting the Sistine Chapel had been put into the Pope's mind by two of Michelangelo's artistic rivals, Bramante and Raphael, who were hoping that, distracted from his forté of sculpture, Michelangelo would either lose the Pope's favor by declining the commission, or simply fail. They were to be sorely disappointed, even if the task of finishing the ceiling to his own exacting standards would tax

Michelangelo immensely. "After four tortured years, more than 400 over life-sized figures, I felt as old and as weary as Jeremiah. I was only 37, yet friends did not recognize the old man I had become," he said at its completion. He began painting toward the end of 1508 and, by the time he finished in 1512, he had painted those 400 life-size figures over an area of more than 5,000 square feet mainly single-handed. Not only did he achieve this but, because he was primarily a sculptor, he had to teach himself many of the techniques necessary for fresco painting.

When the third great left-handed artist of the Italian Renaissance, Raphael (who thought Michelangelo's grim personality resembled that of a "solitary hangman"), saw the unfinished ceiling, it blew him away. He began to incorporate aspects of Michelangelo's style into the paintings he was making in the building next door. The secretive Michelangelo was angry that Pope Julius had allowed his two rivals, Bramante and Raphael, to see the work before it was finished. Such was Michelangelo's competitive pique that, in 1541, long after Raphael was dead, he was still complaining in letters that "everything he knew about art he got from me."

There are many notable features to the Sistine Chapel frescoes. To begin with, for a religious artwork, Michelangelo managed to incorporate a range of pre-Christian classical elements and portraits. There was also a lot of classically inspired nudity, which offended some in the Church but, fortunately not the Pope who had commissioned it, even if some years later another artist was employed to paint loincloths over the genitals. Another interesting feature is that Michelangelo concentrated on the Book of Genesis for his subject matter. Several of the central panels are representations of God creating the world. The whole fresco was, in this sense, a testament to the creation of God, but also to the creative power of the artist.

On the ceiling of the Sistine Chapel, Michelangelo displayed a brilliance that, had it been fully understood, may have seen him accused of heresy. Of all the panels, the most enduring is the *Creation of Adam* which has the image of Adam and God reaching out their hands toward each other. The hand Adam is using to touch God is his left. In medieval iconography it was frequently the devil whose left hand was outstretched. Perhaps Michelangelo's pride and drive to perfection were so powerful that he secretly believed them to be almost diabolical, so he was not merely glorifying, but competing with God in the stakes of creation. This might explain the great tension which pervaded his relationships with the world since, in other respects, he was extremely pious. The Renaissance was a time when the individual began to emerge from the shadow of God, a movement which would culminate in the combination of humanism and faith in science that fueled the Enlightenment 200 years later. Michelangelo's iconography served as a preparation for these shifts in the belief system of European society. Perhaps he remained unaware he was doing this. Still, the one force in his life he was unable to deny was the powerful urge demanding to be expressed by the astonishing capabilities of his left hand.

"MANY YEARS AGO I WENT TO THE VATICAN AND LOOKED AT MICHELANGELO'S FRESCOS IN THE SISTINE CHAPEL. I WAS OVERWHELMED WITH THE FEELING THAT BEFORE MICHELANGELO NO ONE HAD EVER ARTICULATED AND DEPICTED HUMAN PATHOS AS HE DID IN THOSE PAINTINGS. SINCE THEN ALL OF US HAVE UNDERSTOOD OURSELVES JUST THAT LITTLE BIT DEEPER, AND FOR THIS REASON I TRULY FEEL HIS ACHIEVEMENTS ARE AS GREAT AS THE INVENTION OF AGRICULTURE."

WERNER HERZOG, GERMAN FILMMAKER

PAGES 68–69: *THE CREATION OF ADAM*, A DETAIL FROM MICHELANGELO'S SISTINE CHAPEL CEILING, WHICH WAS COMPLETED BETWEEN 1508 AND 1512.

# *Raphael*

THE ITALIAN RENAISSANCE WAS A PINNACLE IN THE HISTORY OF Western civilization that was reached largely with the left hand. Not only were the great artists Leonardo and Michelangelo lefties, but so was their successor, Raphael, who was inspired by them, came to rival Michelangelo and has joined them in the pantheon of Old Masters. This period in history was one of the great lefty peaks of all time and the Renaissance would have been a far lesser event if wasn't for the transformative aesthetics generated by the superior visual and spatial abilities of its southpaw stars.

While Leonardo was an illegitimate child who referred to nature as the ultimate arbiter in matters aesthetic, and lived a rich life of brilliant thought and often unfinished artworks, Michelangelo was a very different type of lefty; one who reacted against the right-handed strictures of parental expectation, and who lived his lefty dream with terrible passion and rage to conquer all the art forms he attempted. Raphael was a different case altogether, a sign of how harmonious left-handers can be if encouraged to develop their lefty abilities. In his short life—he died allegedly after an over-strenuous bout of sex with his mistress at the relatively tender age of 37—Raphael would paint some of the great masterpieces of the Renaissance. But he would also be renowned for his *grazias* (grace), as well as for his paintings and their ease of composition in evoking the Renaissance ideal of human grandeur.

## A CONTENTED LEFTY CHILDHOOD

Raphael was born Raffaello Sanzio in Urbino, a small city state between Rome and Florence. His father was a court factotum who wrote poetry and painted, but was not particularly renowned for his talents in either of these arts. His greatest legacy was perhaps the sensible way he reared his lefty son. To begin with, he believed that children were better served if breastfed

by their natural mothers instead of wet nurses, as Michelangelo and Leonardo both were. Raphael's father also felt that his son should be allowed to grow into his own lefty nature rather than be forced into social hierarchies. The paradox was that this gave Raphael the ease and grace that made him such a brilliant social operator in his adult life. Raphael also benefited from the fact that his father was a painter. Unlike with Michelangelo, there was no struggle for Raphael to be able to pursue the natural gift of his enhanced visual-spatial abilities. He was introduced to art at a very early age, while helping his father out in his studio. His natural aptitude developed easily and in harmony with his family life. Raphael's father was also sufficiently astute to realize that his son possessed more talent than he had himself and, by the time of his death, when he left Raphael an orphan at the age of 11, he had introduced him to the master Perugino, with whom the boy would serve his apprenticeship.

## AN EASEL FULL OF EASE

Like his personality, Raphael's painting was renowned for its grace and ease. This was partly a result of what he learned during his apprenticeship with Perugino, also famous for the gracefulness of his work. But this grace, it must be emphasized, was formed because Raphael's talent was permitted to develop untrammeled. By age 17, when he received his first important commission to paint a chapel altarpiece, Raphael was already being referred to as a master. His early style resembled Perugino in its gentle lyricism, yet outstripped his teacher's by virtue of its naturalism. Again here we are reminded of the right brain's preference for the concrete over the abstract, something the naturalism of the high Renaissance, with its trio of left-handed geniuses, was famous for. In fact, it's interesting to note that in the more abstract world of contemporary art, there don't seem to be as many great left-handed painters as there were in the heyday of realist art.

The highlight of Raphael's naturalism is perhaps his sensitivity toward his subjects. Whereas the faces in Perugino's paintings all tend to look the same, and the subjects are differentiated more by the clothes they wear, in Raphael's work we get the benefits of the lefty's intuition into other people's thoughts, as a result of him being a natural outsider. The people in Raphael's paintings exude a wonderful character and humanity that is conveyed with the kindness that was reflected in Raphael's easy disposition. His work displays a profound, emotionally literate naturalism and possesses a warmer atmosphere than the enigmatic portraits of Leonardo or the anatomically perfect chiseled fury of Michelangelo.

## INFLUENCES

Realizing he had outgrown his master, Perugino, Raphael left Urbino in 1504 and moved to Florence. At the time, Leonardo was dazzling the world with his *Mona Lisa*. Raphael fell under the influence of Leonardo, his devotion to the cause of nature in particular, and his paintings came to be less inhabited by the kind of idealized sweetness

## RAPHAEL'S LEFTY TRAITS

**INTUITIVE** More than Michelangelo or Leonardo, Raphael saw into the emotional lives of his subjects and was able to capture this in his work. His art is most of all remarkable for its human sensitivity, something not acquired by rational means.

**EMPATHETIC** One of the reasons for the particular beauty of Raphael's works is that they resonate with empathy toward the subjects painted. There is a generosity in his paintings, as if the artist seemed to care about the people he painted and understood the frailty of their humanity. His reputation for grace also equates with having an empathetic personality. In his social life he was famous for being able to put people at their ease.

**VISUAL-SPATIAL ABILITY** Raphael's astonishing skills with painting and draftsmanship, as well as his ability to engage with the three-dimensional concerns of architecture, are clear indications that this left-hander was powerfully developed in this area.

OPPOSITE: SELF-PORTRAIT BY RAPHAEL, C.1506.

PAGE 73: *THE TRIUMPH OF GALATEA*, FRESCO, 1512–14.

FOLLOWING PAGES: *THE SCHOOL OF ATHENS*, FRESCO, 1510–11.

MORE THAN ANY OTHER PERSON, ISAAC NEWTON IS RESPONSIBLE for our understanding of the universe today. From inauspicious beginnings as the posthumous child of a Lincolnshire yeoman farmer in England, Newton became a Cambridge University mathematician then went on to become the most famous scientist in the world. His scientific discoveries and inventions include the universal law of gravity, the light spectrum and the reflecting telescope, while in mathematics he was the inventor of differential calculus. He achieved all this in a mass of mental activity—much of the heavy thinking was done in a short burst in his early twenties when he was sequestered at the family farm by the spread of the Black Plague—which effectively ended with a nervous breakdown in 1693 at the age of 50. Yet the price of this brilliance was the possession of a singularly unpleasant personality. Secretive and paranoid, Newton hid his discoveries from the world for 20 years. He had a bad and powerful temper and was also known for the length of time he was capable of holding a grudge.

**YOUNG NEWTON** From an early age Newton displayed a preference for solitude and independent thought. His left-handed mind was different from those around him and the circumstances of his childhood helped to consolidate this. His father died before he was born and when he was three years old his mother remarried an older man. One of the conditions of the marriage was that Isaac be left behind with his grandmother, who lived on a farm some miles outside of the town, where there was no one to play with, since social interaction with the local peasants was forbidden. It was a lonely, unhappy childhood and, in later life, Newton recorded how in a childhood rage he once threatened to burn down the house with his mother and stepfather in it. Abandoned by his mother, Newton's childhood was lived without the usual bonds of familial affection. When he was 10 his stepfather died and his mother returned

home with a half-brother and two half-sisters in tow. Two years later, however, Isaac was packed off again, to a high school in Grantham, a neighboring town, where he boarded with the local apothecary.

This emotionally disconnected childhood allowed Newton's intellect to develop independently. It also meant that he was fueled by rage against the world. If he hadn't had the capability for genius, it's possible Newton might have been a garden variety psychopath. His personality was circumscribed by a strange emotional-intellectual loop whereby rage at the outside world furthered his immersion in the solitary genius of the scientific musings he described as "phantasie." Mathematical thinking was probably an escape from having to deal with his emotions. Genius is often the product of imbalance and, in Newton's case, the left-handed (right-brain) fantasizing, mainly in the language of mathematics—a language as far removed from the expression of emotion as possible—drew him further away from social interaction and reality. For much of his life, Newton was obsessed with alchemy as well as science. While he failed like everyone else in the transmutation of metals, he was far more successful in the transmutation of ordinary human emotions into an intellectual energy that produced some of the most scintillating insights into the construction of nature humans have ever had. It could be said that, unable to solve the problem of himself, he abandoned that exercise and proceeded to solve some of the most vital problems in science.

Many of the lefty geniuses in this book are conspicuous by either their lack of schooling or undisciplined attitude toward the schooling they received. At Grantham, Newton was no exception. In his first year he came 78th out of 80 students. The belief that writing should be carried out with the right hand renders school much more difficult and unnatural for the left-hander. In the case of left-handed geniuses it's also as if the pathways of their own thoughts and the innate knowledge of their differences from others are already too strong, their originality and intuitions too compelling to be reined in with concerns about the relative mediocrity of the received wisdom offered by formal learning. Formal education, however, is about teaching the paths of communication through which individuals come to participate in their cultures. Those who break the conventions can rarely truly belong, and the price for this, as in Newton's case, can be perpetuated isolation. Largely friendless, as a schoolboy Newton preferred to spend his spare time alone, engaged in pursuits such as designing and building working models of water clocks and wooden mills. In the attic of the Grantham apothecarist where he boarded while at school there, he was fond of engraving geometric shapes into the timber wall, a harbinger of where his solitary musings were to take him.

If Newton had already abandoned himself to "phantasie," his mother completely failed to understand this. When he was 16 she hauled him out of school to run the family farm. He proved a complete failure. Already, his only interest in his surroundings were as fuel for his scientific

OPPOSITE: ENGRAVING (AFTER HOUSTON) OF ISAAC NEWTON INVESTIGATING THE PROPERTIES OF LIGHT.

PAGE 81: PORTRAIT OF THE YOUNG ISAAC NEWTON BY AN ANONYMOUS DUTCH ARTIST.

## NEWTON'S LEFTY TRAITS

**INTUITIVE** Newton had the ability to intuit solutions to mathematical problems and provide step-by-step proof in order to check them.

**VISUAL-SPATIAL ABILITY** It took superb visual-spatial skills to work out that the universe was ordered according to the universal law of gravity. One of Newton's main areas of skill was geometry.

**HOT-TEMPERED** Newton was a suspicious man prone to fits of pique. When other scientists dared to disagree with him, he became livid and held grudges for excessively long periods of time.

**SOLITARY** Newton was not close to his family, he had very few friends and displayed an extraordinary lack of interest in sexual matters, which may have been a sign of autism. However, Newton didn't seem to need people and, when forced to interact with them, he could be ruthless. He was admired as the greatest scientist of his era, but this didn't mean he was popular.

**SELF-TAUGHT** Like many other left-handers, his initial school performance was unspectacular. However, he achieved enough for people to recognize his potential. Much of his education, even at Cambridge, was self-directed.

**FANTASIST** Newton used to refer to his mathematical and scientific musings as "phantasie," suggesting that, from a very early age, it was a realm he entered at least partly as an escape from having to deal with the emotional deprivations of his familial world. It would become a pattern that remained with him for the rest of his life and ensured his brilliance was matched with an unbalanced personality. (After all, paranoia is a mode of fantasy too.)

speculations. He neglected his farm work, defied his mother and bullied his half-siblings. He built waterwheels in streams and gained a knowledge of fluid motion while his sheep ate the neighbor's crops. He hid out of sight of the house reading books and day-dreaming. He was fined for allowing his swine to trespass on other people's land. Recognizing both the absurdity of this situation, and Newton's talent, his uncle and former schoolmaster managed to persuade his mother to let him leave Woolsthorpe and return to Grantham to prepare for entry to study at Cambridge. His mother grudgingly acceded and Newton, given this lifeline, became a more determined student and succeeded in gaining entry to Trinity College Cambridge where he enrolled in 1661. At Cambridge, he again proved a somewhat lax and lonely student, skipping lectures and only making one friend. However, his talent was noticed and he began to acquire intellectual acolytes including his professor, Isaac Barrow, who quickly realized his student was smarter than him and generously began to champion his mind.

**PLAGUE AND PURPLE PATCH** Ironically, much of the thinking for Newton's greatest discoveries were completed in the relative isolation of Woolsthorpe some five years later. In 1665 the Black Plague came to London killing one in six Londoners. It swept from village to village toward Cambridge. Students and professors alike abandoned the university for the countryside. Newton returned to Woolsthorpe. This time, however, he wasn't under pressure to become a farmer. As soon as he arrived he set about building himself bookshelves and setting up a study. He took a 1,000-page notebook and set himself problems, gradually expanding his scientific knowledge. Mathematics suited Newton's solitary pursuit of truth, since it gave him the facility to check his intuitions with equations. His geometrical approach to math was a conceptual manifestation of the enhanced visual-spatial abilities often found in left-handers.

During his 20-month sojourn, his family rarely saw Newton and, with the postal service drastically curtailed by the plague, he was operating almost incommunicado. So lost was Newton in his fantasy world of figures and penetrating the secrets of nature, that he didn't bother to sit down for meals and frequently completely forgot to eat until reminded. One day, he was sitting outside in the orchard garden of Woolsthorpe, when an apple fell to the ground. He stared at the apple, reliving its path through the air, his mind in a state of dreamy half-consciousness, puzzling over something still intangible. Then it hit him. The direction the apple fell, along with every other object on this round earth, was toward the earth's center. It wasn't just that the apple fell, but that it tried to go to the earth's center when it did. Now this might seem perfectly logical to us, but Newton's lefty genius saw this in terms of the moon. This was an example of the left-hander's superior capacity for transformational or metaphorical thought—the ability to see one thing in terms of another. For some time Newton had been observing the moon and pondering why it remained in orbit around the earth, and indeed why the earth remained in orbit around the sun. With an intuitive flash, the apple falling in the orchard had given him an answer—gravity.

So what exactly did Newton's brilliant flash of lefty intuition with that apple mean? The observations of astronomers such as Galileo, Copernicus and Kepler had discredited the Aristotlean idea that earth was the center of the universe, but none had been able to come up with a reason why, or for that matter how, the universe was stuck together. Galileo had made advances in the understanding of gravity by timing the descent of the objects of varying weight he dropped from the Leaning Tower of Pisa. Descartes argued that space was composed of invisible matter that rotated around the center of the universe and maintained the relative position of the bodies in it. What Newton saw in the apple was that the earth, by some force, was drawing the apple to it. When he extended this to the moon, he decided that the moon remained in orbit around the earth for the same reason. From this he was able to extrapolate that every object in the universe draws every other object toward it, most likely in proportion to its mass. This theory became known as the universal law of gravity.

**KEEPING SECRETS** It's unlikely that Newton could have achieved this feat of thought if he wasn't a left-handed isolate. One of the most insightful commentaries on the peculiarity of his genius belongs to J. M. Keynes, the great twentieth-century economist, in a lecture he wrote called "Newton the Man:"

> I believe that the clue to his mind is to be found in his unusual powers of continuous concentrated introspection . . . His peculiar gift was the power of holding continuously in his mind a purely mental problem until he had seen straight through it. I fancy his pre-eminence is due to his muscles of intuition being the strongest and most enduring with which a man has ever been gifted. Anyone who has ever attempted pure scientific or philosophical thought knows how one can hold a problem momentarily in one's mind and apply all one's powers of concentration to piercing through it, and how it will dissolve and escape and you find that what you are surveying is a blank. I believe that Newton could hold a problem in his mind for hours and days and weeks until it surrendered to him its secret. Then being a supreme mathematical technician he could dress it up, how you will, for purposes of exposition, but it was his intuition which was pre-eminently extraordinary . . . The proofs, for what they are worth, were, as I have said, dressed up afterwards—they were not the instrument of discovery.

Keynes neatly captures the reason why, as a lefty solitary with immensely powerful muscles of intuition, Newton was able to formulate the universal law of gravity. Without the trajectory of removal from society which had its origins in his childhood, Newton would never have developed the capacity to close out the world in order to concentrate on his problems. What's also remarkable here is that his discoveries were intuition based. The mathematics which justified them was an afterthought, a way of checking, then ultimately of communicating, his discoveries to the larger community.

However, Newton showed considerable reluctance in sharing his discoveries. The first edition of the *Principia Mathematica* which contained the proofs for the universal law of gravity wasn't published until 1685, some 20 years after he had developed it. As Keynes astutely observed, Newton's:

deepest instincts were occult, esoteric, semantic—with profound shrinking from the world, a paralyzing fear of exposing his thoughts, his beliefs, his discoveries in all nakedness to the inspection and criticism of the world . . . Until the second phase of his life, he was a wrapt, consecrated solitary, pursuing his studies by intense intro-spection with a mental endurance perhaps never equaled.

In its creative phase, Newton's mind was a thing of astonishing purity, whose lefty facility for difference, fueled by isolation, was able to main-tain the kind of concentration necessary to penetrate some of the deepest secrets of the universe. Yet the personality that came with it was a fairly twisted piece of work. He reveled in keeping his discoveries a secret, partly because he couldn't stand the thought of being criticized, but just as much because he enjoyed the magical thrill of being the only one to know the way the world truly worked. Newton was convinced of his lefty unique-ness and was prone to celebrating its superior difference as a mode of revenge against the world. When other scientists such as Robert Hooke disagreed with him, he held a grudge until either he was vindicated by their capitulation or they were dead. Newton was blessed and cursed by the fact that with the exception of minor errors he was almost always right.

Being a genius of Newton's order carries a bitter glory; a sentiment that can be found in many of the other great lefty isolates in the pages of this book. The lefty isolate, focused, touchy, paranoid but brilliant is a familiar pattern. Many of the greatest lefties have become addicted to solitude, their minds absorbed in lofty and lefty thoughts without having to make the compromises demanded by interaction with a right-handed world. Yet when they are forced to interact, as they inevitably are, their intuition can desert them. Their mindset is predominantly paranoid inhabiting an emotional field that includes paralyzing insecurity, feelings of persecu-tion and delusions of grandeur, where the fact of their brilliance and its reception by society are never quite at ease.

In 1693, Newton had a nervous breakdown which was roughly contem-poraneous with the end of his creative thinking. Although he was still to publish great works such as his *Opticks*, which would reveal how white light was composed from the color spectrum, they were the fruits of discoveries he had made in his solitary twenties and concealed from the world. Having stopped his creative thinking, Newton became more of a public man, holding the sinecure of Master of the Mint. Between 1703 and his death in 1727 he was the President of the Royal Society where at the same time as elevating it into the primary body of scientific opinion in Europe, he was also prone to unethical behavior, stacking investigative committees against rivals such as Leibniz, with whom Newton competed for being credited with the discovery of differential calculus. The creativity might have gone but the rage, paranoia and solipsistic impulses, which had fueled the great lefty leap of this Rolls Royce mind into the unknown, remained.

## LEFTY LINKS

1. Newton's famous rage, obsessive solitude, competitiveness, secrecy concerning the sharing of his work and general paranoia are all character traits he shared with fellow left-hander, Renaissance artist Michelangelo, who behaved in a similar fashion with his concealment of the ceiling of the Sistine Chapel.

2. The list of left-handed scientists is a long, spectacular and somewhat contentious one. Scientists attributed as left-handers include Aristotle; Newton; Marie Curie; Benjamin Franklin; biologists Linus Pauling and James Watson, the discoverer of DNA; computer scientist Alan Turing; electricity pioneer Nikola Tesla; and physicists Niels Bohr and Richard Feynman. According to Chris McManus in his excellent *Right-Hand Left-Hand* neither Einstein nor Franklin was left-handed. However, educational pressures mean that people who write right-handed can still be left-handed. Einstein's history of poor performance at school followed by self-driven discovery is a pattern often found in left-handers and it has been suggested that if he was not a full lefty, he was at least mixed-handed.

3. When looking at Newton's character, it seems likely he had a form of autism, probably high-functioning Asberger's syndrome. This partly explains his mathematical ability in combination with his lack of emotional engagement with the world. Interestingly, scientific studies have shown that people with autism, if they display handedness, are 60 percent more likely to be left-handed.

# Napoleon Bonaparte

W I T H  A  M I L I T A R Y  R E C O R D  U N E Q U A L E D  B Y  A N Y O N E  E X C E P T  P E R H A P S fellow lefty Alexander the Great, Napoleon Bonaparte is the greatest conqueror in modern history. From insalubrious Corsican beginnings, he climbed the dangerous hierarchies of Revolutionary France to become its leading general, before becoming First Consul and effective ruler of France in 1799. In 1804, he appointed himself hereditary Emperor of France and embarked on a series of military campaigns whose brilliant and surprising battle strategies led to the conquest of most of Europe. These invasions sounded the death knell for the feudal system in Europe. Wherever Napoleon went, he instituted the Napoleonic Code—systematic laws organized around the French Revolution's principles of liberty and equality. However, the cost of maintaining and supplying his massive armies, who remained in an almost constant state of warfare, was immense. His endless urge for battle, failure to translate military prowess into statesmanship, and the impatience that was part of his mercurial lefty temper, led to failed campaigns in Russia and Spain. Weakened by these, Napoleon was eventually defeated by the Sixth Coalition in the Battle of Dresden and exiled to Elba. Less than a year later, however, he escaped and raised an army to fight the Seventh Coalition. He lost the final battle of his career at Waterloo and was imprisoned on the remote Atlantic island, St. Helena, where he died. Despite the series of losses which marked the end of his career, he nonetheless remains the most successful general in the modern world.

**EARLY BONAPARTE** Napoleon was born in 1769, the second son in a family of eight to impoverished Corsican nobility. His father was a lawyer allied with the independence movement, led by Pasquale Paoli, while his mother was a tough nut who never fully subscribed to the success of the child she had given birth to. As a boy, Napoleon was notable for a fiery lefty temper

## LEFTY LINKS

1. One of the reforms Napoleon introduced throughout Europe was the practice of driving on the right-hand side of the road. In feudal times, most traffic had passed on the left. A reason for this was that right-handed horsemen could hold onto their reins with their left hands, while they shook hands with the oncoming traffic, or held their weapons with their right. The "keep to the right" rule was introduced by the Jacobins in 1794. As he built new roads and conquered most of Europe, Napoleon maintained that traffic should pass on the right. It's often said that the reason behind his decision is that, being a left-hander, he wanted the superior defensive position for himself. By the end of the Napoleonic era most of Europe drove on the right. The exceptions were mainly members of the coalition against him: Britain, Russia, Finland, Sweden, Italy and the Austro-Hungarian Empire. Today all of them except for Britain drive on the right: Finland changed in 1858, Russia with the Bolshevik Revolution, Italy and Portugal in the 1920s, while the Austro-Hungarian states changed with their invasion by Hitler. The last state in continental Europe to change was Sweden in 1967.

2. Napoleon shared with Alexander and Caesar the quality of alternating between enlightened despotism and utter ruthlessness. The part of the world which is now Israel, Lebanon, Palestine and Syria seems to have borne the brunt of this across the millennia. At Jaffa, during his Middle Eastern campaign, Napoleon ordered the butchering of 2,000 Turkish soldiers who were trying to surrender. His army then embarked on a massacre of the civilian inhabitants, which lasted for several days. Following this, Napoleon ordered the execution of a further 3,000 Turkish prisoners. It was a display of cold-blooded ruthlessness, reminiscent of Alexander's mass crucifixion after the Siege of Tyre. Both acts were designed to strike fear into the hearts of the enemy.

that remained with him throughout his life. Although a year younger, and much smaller, he often beat up his brother Giuseppe. His nickname as a kid was *rabulione*, which meant the one who meddles in everything.

Unlike many of the left-handers in this book, Napoleon showed an excellent aptitude for formal education. He first went to school when he was five and was taught by the local nuns. Even at this young age, he showed a precocious talent for mathematics, a faculty in which left-handers often excel. At the age of eight he went to a local farmer's mill and spent the day calculating its production. He was exceedingly good at doing math in his head, a talent that would serve him well, especially when having to form strategies and move armies in the heat of the battle. As France had bought Corsica in 1768, Napoleon was eligible for a scholarship granted to impoverished children of the French nobility. It offered training for either the military or the priesthood. In 1778, Napoleon was enrolled in the military school while his brother Giuseppe was enrolled for the priesthood.

After a preparatory year, where he learned French, Napoleon spent six years at the military school in Brienne, the only Corsican among boys from some of the wealthiest families in Europe. Like many lefties, this would only have confirmed his pre-existing sense of difference from the status quo. It undoubtedly spurred Napoleon's ambition. Following Brienne, he went to the elite Ecole Militare where he specialized in artillery and graduated in one year from a course that normally took several. At the age of 16, his formal education was complete and Napoleon became a second lieutenant in the French Army.

**YOUNG AND BONEY** One of the reasons Napoleon chose to join the artillery was because his mathematical skills were strong, and gave him an advantage in working out the angles, trajectories and ranges essential to accurate bombardment. Napoleon's mathematical ability was augmented by the left-handed, visual-spatial gift of being able to visualize terrain from the often erratic contents of maps. It gave him a major strategic advantage over other officers, in that he was able to accurately place his artillery. He could also calculate the time it would take to bring an army to a given place. He would use this knowledge time and time again to split the armies of the numerically superior coalition forces that fought against him.

After graduation from military school, Napoleon continued to educate himself in the affairs of the world through a course of self-determined reading. He also took leave from the French Army to go and fight with Paoli in Corsica. However, the two ended up falling out and the entire Bonaparte family had to leave Corsica in a hurry.

Napoleon achieved his first actual battle success at the siege of Toulon in 1793. Although only a captain, he devised a plan that eventually crushed the British and Royalist hold over the city. He used his strategic acumen to formulate a way of breaking the ring of British artillery around the city. In doing so, he surprised the enemy, who had boasted of their position's impregnability by calling it a "Little Gibraltar." Napoleon bombarded the British positions and was wounded in the thigh by a British bayonet in the ensuing battle, which ended in a naval evacuation by the British and Royalist forces. His brilliance at Toulon saw Napoleon promoted from Captain to Brigadier General in one hit. He became a marked favorite of the Jacobin leader, Robespierre, and returned to Paris where his political star also began to rise. It almost fell under the guillotine soon after with the denunciation and decapitation of Robespierre in 1794, but Napoleon was lucky. Although arrested as Robespierre's protégé, he was quietly released, perhaps out of recognition of his potential for assisting the nation with his prowess on the battlefield.

Napoleon further enhanced his military reputation through his tactics in battle against the Austrians at Dego, Italy, in 1794. He returned to Paris and began to agitate for greater responsibility. His third success after Toulon and Dego came when he successfully stood down a 30,000-person mob of malcontents by using grapeshot fired from his cannons in Paris. This battle is a good example of Napoleon's intuitive know-how. He believed that if you could inspire fear in the enemy, then the battle was more than half-way won. He used grapeshot because it would hit a lot of people, creating fear and bloodshed, yet with insufficient fatalities to turn it into an incident of mass martyrdom that might be used against him in the future for the purposes of revenge. As a consequence of this adroit handling of the situation, he found a new patron, Director Barras. When he applied to become commander of an army to invade Italy in 1796, he got the job. He also got Barras' former mistress, Josephine, another left-hander, as a wife.

Napoleon's reasons for pursuing the Italian command (other than his innately martial instincts) were largely based on his interpretation of the life of his fellow lefty Julius Caesar. Because of his Gallic campaign, Caesar had been able to build a power base independent of the swirling political allegiances of Rome. When he returned from Gaul with a triumphant army, it massively enhanced his popularity with the people, not least because of the riches that returned with him. Importantly, when Pompey militated against him, Caesar had a loyal army and a base outside of Rome that he could use to advance his cause.

With the political situation so volatile in Paris, this was a lesson Napoleon took heed of. When Napoleon took over his Italian army, it was a motley, ill-disciplined and poorly fed assemblage. But, like Caesar, he knew how to pull it into shape. Through conquering territory, the army was able to feed itself. Italy was also full of loot and Napoleon earned the loyalty of his men by giving them a share of it, and setting up a system by which these gains could be remitted easily to their families. It was in this campaign where his men nicknamed him the "Little Corporal," to indicate their affection for a leader who looked after their interests and behaved without the usual airs and graces of the mostly aristocratic military leaders. Napoleon also began to acquire the personal wealth that was necessary for

3. For intellectuals such as Beethoven, stuck in despotic regimes like the Austro-Hungarian Empire, Napoleon's rise and the reforms he instigated felt like a breath of fresh air. After the turmoil of the Terror, it appeared that he might be capable of rescuing the ideals of the French Revolution. For this reason, his military actions did not always arouse complete hostility in the countries at which they were directed. However, disillusionment set in when Napoleon crowned himself hereditary Emperor of France. Beethoven, who had planned to dedicate his *Third Symphony* to Napoleon, was so furious that he scratched the Frenchman's name out and wrote in the name of one of his aristocratic Austrian patrons instead.

4. One of the main reasons for Napoleon's ultimate defeat was that his brilliant strategical insights into battle were almost entirely restricted to land. As such, the British Navy were able to gain nautical superiority over the French and use this to interfere with troop movements and block supplies. The key battle is the 1805 Battle of Trafalgar, where the British were led by left-handed admiral, Horatio Nelson. Nelson was originally right-handed but, in 1797, while in command of four ships trying to attack French-allied Spanish assets in the Canary Islands, his right arm was hit by a cannonball and had to be amputated. Nelson prepared to retire from the navy, writing: "A left-handed admiral will never again be considered as useful; therefore the sooner I get to a very humble cottage the better, and make room for a sounder man to serve the state." Before this he had also lost the sight in his right eye. The British Admiralty, however, thought differently, and Nelson continued to harass the French Navy, until heading the decisive victory at Trafalgar during which he was killed.

PAGE 89: PORTRAIT OF NAPOLEON IN HIS STUDY, 1812, BY JACQUES LOUIS DAVID.

## NAPOLEON'S LEFTY TRAITS

**INTUITIVE** Napoleon knew how to inspire fear in his enemies and was renowned for his amazing instincts about the right time to attack. He also had an excellent understanding of the needs of, and how to maintain the loyalty of, his men.

**VISUAL-SPATIAL ABILITY** Combined with his mathematical ability, this skill enabled Napoleon to visualize a battlefield from a map and to organize his artillery with great precision.

**LATERAL THINKING** Evidence of this trait can be found in Napoleon's battle stratagems, and also in the way that he constructed his own propaganda, such as the Egyptian scientific expedition.

**HOT-TEMPERED** Like many great left-handers, this was Napoleon's Achilles heel. His temper was legendary and was accompanied by an insatiable love of war, as well as the impatience that played a major part in his undoing.

**ICONOCLASTIC** Napoleon's Enlightenment-based reforms, including the Napoleonic Code, made a serious contribution to the end of feudalism in Europe.

**FANTASIST** In his early life Napoleon wrote fiction and history, but it is perhaps his dream of glory, and inability to see its limits, which mark him as a man with a fantastic streak to his imagination.

his own political ambition, enabling him, for instance, to start his own newspaper and talk himself up, while some of Italy's greatest artworks and cultural artefacts were shipped to Paris, where their display in museums such as the Louvre became a measure of national glory.

The Italian campaign is often considered Napoleon's greatest. He defeated both the Austrians and the army of the Papal States and took control of a huge swathe of Italy. His army captured 160,000 prisoners and 2,000 cannons. Battles were won by surprise and deception. He was a pioneer in the field of military intelligence, deploying new technology such as the Chappe semaphore, a coded system of displayed rods at angles which dramatically increased the speed at which information could travel. Napoleon had the lateral gift of being able to instinctively apply his impressive book knowledge of military matters to the concrete situation of the battlefield and visualize the outcome. He rather arrogantly claimed, "I have fought sixty battles and I have learned nothing which I did not know at the beginning." To a certain extent, this was true.

## FIRST CONSUL TO SELF-CROWNING

In 1798, Napoleon followed the trail of his left-handed military heroes, Alexander and Caesar, to Egypt, where he achieved massive propaganda success by incorporating a scientific expedition into his mission. The expedition discovered many Ancient Egyptian artefacts, including the Rosetta Stone, which enabled French scholars to translate the Egyptian hieroglyphs, without which the story of Ramses the Great would never have become known. The results of the Egyptian campaign were mixed. There were brilliant victories, but also defeats, mainly due to the prevalence of bubonic plague among his troops and British naval superiority. (Napoleon never really got his head around the importance of the navy, which is ultimately one of the reasons why he was defeated.)

In 1799, however, with Egypt left as unfinished business, Napoleon was summoned back to France, where the situation was precarious. There was a threat of invasion by the members of the Second Coalition, comprised of Britain, Austria, Russia and the Ottoman Empire. The Directory which was running France was incompetent and out of favor with the public. One of the directors, Sieyes, approached Napoleon for military support in a coup. On November 9, 1799, they seized control and Napoleon, like Caesar, became a member of a ruling triumvirate. His title was First Consul of France.

Napoleon's period as First Consul was relatively free from war and in this period he, as ever restlessly intelligent, instituted wide-ranging reforms to the law, education and banking systems, sewers and roads, which earned him a reputation for spreading the values of the Enlightenment. The intelligentsia, who still lived under despotic rule throughout Europe, viewed him as a potential savior and disseminator of the ideals of the French Revolution.

They were disappointed. In 1804, using an assassination plot against him to argue the need for dynastic inheritance to ensure political stability, Napoleon declared himself hereditary Emperor of France and it wasn't long before the Napoleonic Wars had begun in earnest.

**WAR WAR WAR** In 1805, Britain, Austria and Russia united against Napoleon in the Third Coalition. At the Battle of Ulm, Napoleon used a brilliant and rapid wheeling maneuver to isolate the Austrian Army of General Mack. It was an example of how his visual-spatial intelligence, and ability to move his army at speed, proved superior to the opposing forces. On December 2, 1805, Napoleon enjoyed his greatest victory at Austerlitz. It was again a masterpiece of strategical thinking. With his supply lines stretched, Napoleon was hoping the Austrians and Russians, led by Tsar Alexander, would come to him and engage him in battle. In order to facilitate this, he deliberately weakened his army's right flank in order to create the illusion of vulnerability. He hoped the enemy would notice, and find it too tempting to resist. Once they were attacking the right flank, Napoleon then planned to mount an assault through the center of the Allied Forces, which were thinned out due to the attack on his right flank. It was a fiercely fought battle which lasted for over nine hours before the French forces prevailed. As the Allied troops retreated over the ice, Napoleon displayed his brilliant ruthlessness and ability to surprise by ordering his cannons to fire at the ice and break it up so that the enemy would be drowned. Many did. The Allies lost 27,000 out of 75,000 men, while Napoleon only lost 9,000 from a smaller army of 67,000. In three months, the French were in Vienna.

# *Beethoven*

WHEN WE SPEAK OF TORTURED GENIUS, THE NAME BEETHOVEN IS NEVER far from our lips. Some have argued that this German composer, who produced some of the world's most enduring musical works, despite suffering from increasing deafness from the age of 27, is the greatest mind humanity has ever known. While this may be open to debate, it nonetheless comes as no surprise to hear that Beethoven was a lefty. He revolutionized classical music through the introduction of Romanticism and organic structure, thereby making possible the careers of many of the great composers who followed him. With his unruly mane of silver hair, disheveled dress, foul temper and conspicuous eccentricity, this left-handed iconoclast is one of the first images to appear in our minds when we think of the tempestuous lives of great artists.

**YOUNG LUDWIG** Ludwig van Beethoven was born in Bonn in West Germany in 1770. At the time, Bonn was the capital of the Electorate of Cologne, a principality significant for being a trading center and also because its Elector was one of the princes responsible for electing the Holy Roman Emperor. Beethoven was a third-generation musician. His grandfather, also called Ludwig, was the master of the Court Chapel choir and enjoyed a reputation as a fine bass singer. Beethoven's father, Johann, who was an alcoholic, had been less successful, but was still a court musician who sang and played the violin and clavier.

Beethoven showed early signs of being a prodigy, but was hampered to some extent by his father's ambivalence toward his talent. At times Johann lauded his son's precocity yet at others he tended to resent it. On one occasion, according to an account by his childhood neighbors Gottfried and Cäcilia Fischer, Johann admonished his son for improvising—a classic case of mediocre talent repressing the lefty individuality of the great. Nonetheless, his father arranged Beethoven's first performance at the age

LEFTY LINKS

of seven, with the hope of inviting comparisons with the child prodigy of the previous generation, Mozart.

Like many of the great left-handers in these pages, Beethoven ceased his formal schooling while relatively young. He went to a Latin primary school until he was 10 but did not go on to the Gymnasium (German for high school). The originality of Beethoven's lefty mind perhaps profited from his lack of formal schooling. Certainly, by the time he went to Vienna aged 22 and studied with Haydn, he had strong opinions which made him resistant to Haydn's teachings. The fact that he was sufficiently strong and willful to resist convention, even when being taught by a great composer, was a clear sign of his individuality and brilliance.

**HEARING PROBLEMS** When he was about 27 years old and still fairly new in Vienna, Beethoven began to notice a constant ringing in his ears. At the time, he was already regarded as arguably the best and certainly the most daring concert pianist in Vienna, and his renown as a classical composer was growing. The ringing worsened and, in 1802, his doctor prescribed a sojourn in the rural quiet of Heiligenstadt, an hour by carriage from Vienna, to allow his hearing a chance to recover. Around this time, Beethoven had expressed dissatisfaction with the direction his music was taking. Previously his composition had been largely in the classical tradition, whose expression had reached a pinnacle with Mozart and Haydn. There were signs, however, that Beethoven wanted to leave this affiliation and create something new.

While he was recuperating at Heiligenstadt, Beethoven had an existential crisis. Although he was enjoying the peacefulness of the countryside, his hearing wasn't getting any better. In fact it got worse; a situation that provoked Beethoven into a serious contemplation of suicide as can be seen from the Heiligenstadt Testimony which he wrote to his brothers but never sent:

> O ye men who think or say that I am malevolent, stubborn or misanthropic, how greatly do ye wrong me, you do not know the secret causes of my seeming, from childhood my heart and mind were disposed to the gentle feelings of good will, I was even ever eager to accomplish great deeds, but reflect now that for six years I have been a hopeless case, aggravated by senseless physicians, cheated year after year in the hope of improvement, finally compelled to face the prospect of a lasting malady (whose cure will take years or, perhaps, be impossible), born with an ardent and lively temperament, even susceptible to the diversions of society, I was compelled early to isolate myself, to live in loneliness, when I at times tried to forget all this, O how harshly was I repulsed by the doubly sad experience of my bad hearing, and yet it was impossible for me to say to men speak louder, shout, for I am deaf. Ah how could I possibly admit such an

1. Both Beethoven and Leonardo profited from the fact that their formal schooling ended when they were about 10. It affected their attitudes toward their art dramatically. Instead of looking to the masters who preceded them as the ultimate authority, they preferred to make nature their ultimate authority. Leonardo placed his priority on the primacy of the natural world as perceived by the eye. Beethoven appealed to nature through the Romantic belief that creativity was an organic process that intuitively penetrated the essence of nature.

2. The left-hander with perhaps the greatest influence on Beethoven's life was Napoleon Bonaparte, who he once thought the greatest man in Europe—only to change his mind when the Corsican betrayed the French Revolution by declaring himself Emperor of France.

3. Other great classical composers and musicians who were left-handed include Carl Philipp Emanuel Bach, Sergei Rachmaninoff and the brilliant, eccentric Canadian piano virtuoso Glenn Gould.

4. One area of the orchestra where you won't see much left-handed playing is in the string section. It's the musical equivalent of lefties and righties bumping each other at the dinner table. Perhaps this is the reason why Beethoven, who played both violin and piano, was reputed to be a mediocre violin player yet, until the onset of deafness, was one of the greatest piano virtuosos of his time.

OPPOSITE: PORTRAIT OF BEETHOVEN AFTER A PAINTING BY CHRISTIAN HORNEMAN, 1803.

PAGE 101: IN 2003 THE MANUSCRIPT FOR BEETHOVEN'S NINTH SYMPHONY WAS AUCTIONED AT SOTHEBY'S IN LONDON AND SOLD FOR A RECORD $3.5 MILLION.

## BEETHOVEN'S LEFTY TRAITS

**INTUITIVE** As a Romantic composer, Beethoven introduced individual emotion to music which transcended the formalism of the classical music that preceded his.

**HOT-TEMPERED** Beethoven's temper made him difficult to deal with from an early age, as is evident from his failed relationship with Haydn. Undoubtedly his increasing deafness did nothing to improve this. As he lost the ability to participate in conversations, he was forced to rely on the direct expression of emotion and conversation books (blank notebooks in which people would write their questions).

**SOLITARY** Again, Beethoven's deafness caused him to become isolated from the world. This was also compounded by the fact that Beethoven never married. Throughout his life, Beethoven had the unfortunate habit of falling in love with socially unattainable women. Although the great age of Romantic genius was beginning to flower, in Beethoven's time musicians still had a low social standing. His love life was disastrous, which fed his fury at the poor deal his genius had been offered by life.

**ICONOCLASTIC** Forget rock music, Beethoven was perhaps the most iconoclastic musician who ever lived. He completely revolutionized orchestral music, turning it into a stunning vehicle for the expression of tumultuous individualistic emotion.

**EXPERIMENTAL** This can be seen in the way that Beethoven adapted the musical forms he worked within. His many successful experiments included the dramatic elongation of the symphonic form, the incorporation of literature into his music by the use of choral singing, and the use of unconventional juxtapositions between the emotional textures of a symphony's movements.

OPPOSITE: BEETHOVEN'S MUSIC SYMBOLIZED THE TRANSITION BETWEEN EIGHTEENTH-CENTURY CLASSICISM AND NINETEENTH-CENTURY ROMANTICISM.

infirmity in the one sense which should have been more perfect in me than in others, a sense which I once possessed in highest perfection, a perfection such as few surely in my profession enjoy or have enjoyed . . . Forced already in my 28th year to become a philosopher, O it is not easy, less easy for the artist than for anyone else—Divine One thou lookest into my inmost soul, thou knowest it, thou knowest that love of man and desire to do good live therein ...

## THE THIRD SYMPHONY "EROICA"

Following this crisis, Beethoven's music became more daring, as if he had faced his fears and no longer felt beholden to anyone but himself. Much of the emotion of his determination to persevere, despite the handicap of encroaching deafness, is captured in the Third Symphony, also known as the Heroic Symphony, or 'Eroica', which Beethoven mostly composed during 1803. There had been no symphony like it before and, when it was first performed in 1805, it seriously divided its audience between those who found much of it senseless and fragmented bombast, versus those who saw a new kind of holistic brilliance embedded in its massive and often disruptive momentum. Some even argued that it would take the listening public a generation to develop sufficiently to fully understand such a masterpiece. The importance of Beethoven as the first Romantic composer cannot be underestimated. The Romantics valued music extremely highly, believing that since music was immaterial (without physical form) it was the art form most capable of expressing the individual's soul.

So what was revolutionary about Symphony No. 3? To begin with, it was half as long again as any symphony that had gone before it. From the enormous first movement with its 691 bars, it becomes clear that Beethoven's Third is responsible for taking the symphonic poem to an all new epic scale. With its radical disjunctions in mood between the funeral march of the second movement and the jaunty scherzo of the third, it introduced a new emotional palate into music, which had previously been constrained by the pursuit of formal elegance. The disjunctions of mood within and between movements helped create a sense of elevated personal expression, as if the listener was in direct communication with the soul of the composer—an effect not discernible in predecessors such as Mozart and Haydn. The deployment of an extra horn in the orchestra helped build a romantic sense of grandeur, which presages the enormous orchestras employed by later composers such as Mahler and Wagner.

The Third's form showed a strong left-handed disregard for the conventions of received musical wisdom. At the time, one critic derided it as "a colossal piling of ideas." Yet much of the magnificent tension in the music is a result of how Beethoven was able to synthesize several powerful narratives—his own crisis, the rise of Napoleon Bonaparte and the Prometheus legend of Greek mythology—to drive the Third along. Such

attempts to seek synthesis were very much a part of the Romantic view of the world, which placed emphasis on the holistic and organic, in opposition to the piece-by-piece linearity of scientific thought. It is unsurprising that the instigation of these Romantic approaches came from a left-hander, since holistic thinking tends to be more of a right-brain activity, while step-by-step logic is more the domain of the left. Furthermore left-handers tend to have greater communication between the two hemispheres of their brains than do right-handers. This is particularly useful in music where the right hemisphere of the brain tends to be responsible for pitch and melody, while the left is responsible for complex rhythms.

Critics have long pondered the reason why the funeral march of the second movement is followed by a joyous scherzo and finale. An obvious reading is of Beethoven confronting his darkest fears at Heiligenstadt then feeling release once he has decided to keep going. Another possible interpretation is that the symphony is about Napoleon rescuing the ideals of the French Revolution. According to a number of contemporary sources, Beethoven originally intended the Third to be dedicated to his fellow left-hander, Napoleon Bonaparte. At the time Bonaparte, as First Consul of France, was widely considered to have rescued the French Revolution and its ideals of liberty, equality and fraternity from the excesses of the Terror, the indiscriminate bloodbath that came with the fanatical leadership of Robespierre. For Beethoven, living in the largely benign but retrograde political environment of the Austro-Hungarian empire, the values of the French Revolution were attractive, as they were to most artists and intellectuals of the period. Yet there was also disillusionment. When Beethoven heard that Napoleon had proclaimed himself Emperor of France he was outraged. He ripped up the title page with the dedication to Napoleon and the Third instead was dedicated to one of his patrons, Prince Lobkowitz. There was a sting in the tail as well. Along with dedication were the words "composed to celebrate the memory of a great man." Napoleon, of course, was still alive.

Other listeners to the Third have noticed thematic similarities with Beethoven's ballet *The Creatures of Prometheus*, Opus 43, first performed in 1801. In the Greek legend, Prometheus is punished by the gods for giving humans fire. He is chained to a rock and an eagle comes every day and eats his liver. At night the organ regenerates and the agony begins all over again. This tale of the rebel (perhaps Prometheus was a lefty too), who breaks the divine rules in order to bring about an improvement of the human condition, resonated strongly with the Romantics. In his ballet, Beethoven changed the story so Prometheus is executed for his transgression then later reborn. It's easy to imagine how Beethoven, having been in a suicidal state because of his deafness, only to emerge from it to write greater music than ever, could have identified with a myth in which a man is punished by the gods for his betterment of humankind.

OPPOSITE: A PORTRAIT OF BEETHOVEN FROM C.1800, WHEN HE WAS ABOUT 30 YEARS OF AGE.

## WAS BEETHOVEN REALLY A LEFTY?

As with many figures in history, it is often difficult to tell whether people were lefties or righties. There are undoubtedly people who, for reasons of discrimination, preferred to be known as righties rather than lefties. It is also generally assumed that if there is no mention of a person's handedness then they are right-handed. With pre-photographic cases, such as Beethoven's, the territory is murky. While a number of portraits show him as being right-handed, this has to be balanced against the testimony of Beethoven's friend, companion and first biographer, the violinist Anton Schindler, who claimed that Beethoven was a lefty. As a biographer, Schindler was notoriously inventive—but mostly in the cause of protecting Beethoven's posterity. Therefore, it is unlikely that he would have invented Beethoven's left-handedness. It is more likely the portraits are a misrepresentation due to the fact that Beethoven was a reluctant sitter. One portrait of Beethoven with a pen in his right hand, painted by Joseph Karl Stieler in 1819–20, is often used as evidence for Beethoven's right-handedness. Stieler claimed he was the only painter Beethoven agreed to sit for, and the painting was understood to be a very good likeness. However, the hands had to be painted from memory, as Beethoven could not be persuaded to stay for the required number of sittings. Perhaps Stieler assumed that Beethoven was right-handed, or maybe he chose to portray Beethoven as right-handed because the cultural stigmatization of left-handedness might undermine the grandeur of his subject.

**THE NINTH OR CHORAL SYMPHONY** Beethoven's Third marked a break with symphonic tradition. Yet Beethoven's most famous symphony, and his last, is probably the Ninth, or Choral Symphony. This work was also powerfully iconoclastic. It is an immoveable brick in the symphonic canon that every composer post-Beethoven has in some way had to deal with. With its radical setting of Schiller's poem *Ode to Joy* in the final movement, the Ninth was the first symphony to use choral singing—and to stunning effect. The Ninth has been used for national anthems, and the *Ode to Joy* movement (with altered lyrics) is the official anthem of the European Union. It has even had an effect on recent technology. The CD was originally designed to hold 74 minutes of music, because this was the length of Beethoven's Ninth Symphony.

The Ninth's impact on other composers was immense, sending some such as Schubert and Mendelssohn in search of texts to use to structure their works. Others such as Mahler and Wagner were inspired by the sheer grandeur of the music and the sound of such a large orchestra augmented with voices. Wagner wrote in 1846 that, "It is wonderful how the master makes the arrival of the human voice and tongue a positive necessity, by this awe-inspiring recitative of the bass strings; almost breaking the bounds of absolute music already, it stems the tumult of the other instruments with its eloquence, insisting on decision, and passes at last into a songlike theme whose simple stately flow bears with it, one by one, the other instruments, until it swells into a mighty flood." The French composer Claude Debussy wrote, "It [the Ninth] is the most triumphant example of the molding of an idea to the preconceived form; at each leap forward there is a new delight, without either effort or appearance of repetition; the magical blossoming, so to speak, of a tree whose leaves burst forth simultaneously. Nothing is superfluous in this stupendous work." Here we get the sense of the Ninth as a supremely Romantic achievement of organic creation, left-handed in its holistic approach to composition and its iconclastic form.

The Ninth is even more astonishing when you consider that when Beethoven composed it he was completely deaf. Although he introduced radical new elements to the symphony, he heard none of them, except in his head. The symphony's composition was based entirely upon Beethoven's memories of sound.

At its premiere in May 1824 in the Kärntnertortheater in Vienna. Beethoven joined the Kapellmeister and conductor Ignaz Umlauf on the stage. Because he was deaf, Beethoven was unable to hear the orchestra and for this reason Umlauf instructed the musicians not to pay any attention to the composer. As the orchestra played, Beethoven, nonetheless conducted with great emotion. So carried away was he with the music in his head that when the orchestra finished the piece, he continued to conduct. Eventually one of the singers turned him round to face a bemused audience who had already begun to applaud. He looked like a madman, and the applause was polite until it dawned on them that he had written the work without being able to hear. In sympathy and wonder at the achievement, the first round of applause became a second, then a third, fourth and fifth. In order that Beethoven could comprehend this they waved their handkerchiefs up and down. The maestro was profoundly moved. Three rounds of applause were generally reserved only for the Imperial Family, and after the fifth, the chief of police stood up and told the audience to desist from any further praise. Nonetheless it was a fitting tribute to an iconoclastic left-handed genius, who quite literally spent most of his life marching to the beat of his own drum.

PLASTER CASTS OF BEETHOVEN'S HANDS, PROBABLY MADE WHILE THE COMPOSER WAS STILL ALIVE.

# *Queen Victoria*

WHEN QUEEN VICTORIA INHERITED THE THRONE OF BRITAIN AGED 18, it was in a fairly dire state. Following the long reign of mad King George III, the crown had passed to two of his sons, the high-living George IV, and William IV, whose reign saw considerable dimunition in the powers of the monarch. Aided by her left-handed abilities of intuition, empathy and the capacity to be at ease in times of great transformation, Victoria took control of her destiny and turned a monarchy that was losing popularity with the people into one of Europe's most beloved, while showing a political acumen and tact that helped guide Britain through the tumultuous changes of the nineteenth century. Her rule coincided with the apex of the British Empire and, by the time of her death in 1901, her dominion covered over a quarter of the habitable area of the world and her subjects numbered 400 million. Queen for 63 years, Victoria was the longest-reigning monarch in British history. Even today, the word "Victorian" connotes a particular cultural flavor—sentimentality, an obsession with death and excessive mourning, a moral rigidity (at least in outward appearances), and the illusion of solidity in a world of constant flux. This emanated from Victoria herself, but also represented the values and beliefs of Britain's burgeoning middle class, who had grown wealthy on the profits of the Empire and relative peace, whose tastes the Queen shared and represented.

**PRINCESS VICTORIA** Victoria was the only daughter of Edward, Duke of Kent (the third son of George III) and the widowed Princess Regent of Leinigen, Victoire. As with many of the royal family, her father was rather broke and, as a consequence, was forced to live on the European continent where the cost of living was cheaper. However, the sons of George were making a poor show of producing legitimate heirs and when the 50-year-old Edward found out his young wife was pregnant, he insisted the baby be born in England.

Edward died some eight months later and Victoria's mother was left saddled with her husband's debts in a country where she couldn't speak the language and wasn't completely sure whether she was welcome. George IV reluctantly provided rooms for mother and child in Kensington Palace where Victoria grew up speaking only German until the age of three. Her childhood was not that of a typical princess. Due to her poor financial status, she was forced to share a room with her mother and to eat the cheapest cuts of meat, such as mutton.

Victoria's childhood was also fairly isolated. She mainly lived among the German ladies her mother kept as her retinue and, with the exception of the children of her mother's advisor, John Conroy, she had no one to play with. In some ways her childhood resembles that of fellow lefty Isaac Newton, who also suffered from the social isolation of being from a higher class, and therefore distant, to those around him. She didn't have fond memories of her childhood. In 1858, she wrote to her eldest daughter:

> I had led a very unhappy life as a child—had no scope for my very violent feelings of affection—had no brothers or sisters to live with—never had a father—from my unfortunate circumstances was not on a comfortable or at all intimate or confidential feeling with my mother …

Like Newton, Victoria found solace from her unhappy childhood in intellectual pursuits, though she didn't share his incommunicative tendencies. The princess was lucky enough to have two good tutors and a facility for languages, which would serve her in good stead since her children and grandchildren later populated most of the thrones of Europe. At the age of five, Victoria acquired a governess, Fräulein Lehzen, who initially was appalled by the outbursts of temper from the little princess, yet observed that she always told the truth and therefore was fond of her. Lehzen declared that she had never seen such a passionate and naughty child. This, combined with Victoria's instinct for truthfulness, is a sure sign of the instinctive left-handed rage which can emerge from the feeling of injustice that comes from being out of kilter with the world. It was a rage that, once she was monarch, she was able to rein in through a combination of self-awareness and powerful self-discipline. Under the stewardship of her governess, Victoria went from a recalcitrant student to an excellent one. As she got older, she acquired a tutor, the Reverend George Davies, who taught her subjects considered more fit for a prince than a princess, such as law, history and other real world matters, such as the technology of the Industrial Revolution which was driving Britain's prosperity. Novels, considered decadent, were banned, though she was allowed to read poetry. By the time she inherited the throne, Victoria could almost be considered a tomboy of the mind.

**QUEEN VICTORIA** Victoria was only 18 when she became Queen upon the death of William IV in 1837, just old enough to rule on her own without her mother being installed as regent. Physically she was far from

OPPOSITE: COLORED LITHOGRAPH BY S. P. DENNING, OF PRINCESS VICTORIA AT FOUR YEARS OLD.

PAGE 111: QUEEN VICTORIA AT HER WRITING DESK, C.1878. SPEAKING ONLY GERMAN UNTIL THE AGE OF THREE, VICTORIA LATER BECAME CONVERSANT IN ENGLISH, CHINESE, GREEK, ITALIAN AND FRENCH.

FOLLOWING PAGES: AN ILLUSTRATION FROM 1887, DURING VICTORIA'S GOLDEN JUBILEE, PICTURING HER AT THE START OF HER REIGN IN 1837 AND AS SHE APPEARED 50 YEARS LATER.

E. GRIVAT

## VICTORIA'S LEFTY TRAITS

**INTUITIVE** Victoria performed best in one-on-one situations and had a talent for finding wise counsel and cultivating passionate friendships which belied the severe countenance of her public face post-Albert. She also proved to be an astute match-maker when it came to marrying her children and grandchildren into the Royal families of Europe.

**EMPATHETIC** Her ability to understand others proved a great asset in the popularity of Victoria's monarchy, especially in the overseas sections of the British Empire and abroad.

**HOT-TEMPERED** As a child the princess was famous for her stubbornness and temper and, although as an adult she achieved self-control, signs of this aspect of her character can be found throughout her long life. Some of her hot-headedness manifested itself in her passion for war.

**ICONOCLASTIC** While the idea of an iconoclastic monarch is perhaps paradoxical, in many ways Victoria broke the mold. Her liberality and tolerance were ideal for an age where the middle class were usurping the aristocracy as the driving force of the nation, and where many of her subjects inhabited foreign lands. The strength of her passion and mourning for Albert was also somewhat iconoclastic given that most royal marriages were made for dynastic rather than romantic reasons. The persistence of her mourning can almost be construed as rebellion against the rules of life.

**FANTASIST** Victoria was possessed of romantic and sentimental streaks which showed themselves most dramatically in the mourning for her husband Albert.

prepossessing as a monarch. She was just under 5 feet tall and on the way to becoming rather stout. Still, she immediately made her mark on the monarchy by asserting her independence from her power-hungry mother and her ambitious advisor John Conroy. Whereas William IV had attempted to remove Lord Melbourne as Prime Minister, Victoria made him her political intimate. Like Joan of Arc, Victoria had an instinctive ability to bend powerful men into believing in her although, unlike Joan, she did have the advantage of her crown. Her masculine education gave her a base from which she could engage with Melbourne, a Liberal whose politics were tolerant and slightly world weary. A widower who knew society and whose wife had had an affair with the poet Byron, Melbourne was enchanted by the enthusiasm Victoria showed for her new job and spent a great deal of time educating her. He wasn't just her Prime Minister but also functioned as an informal private secretary, dinner and after-dinner companion. Victoria had chosen her mentor wisely and his tolerance would inform the rest of her reign.

Melbourne's centrality in Victoria's life was displaced by the Queen's marriage to Albert, son of the Duke of Saxe-Coburg-Gotha, in 1840. On Melbourne's encouragement, Victoria had proposed to Albert as his inferior rank prevented him from doing so. Victoria and Albert proved a good match, a happy and mostly harmonious combination of left-handed female and right-handed male. In addition to having nine children, they effectively ruled (constitutionally, of course) as a team, although Parliament resisted granting Albert any actual titles for a long time. Whereas Queen Victoria was passionate, stubborn and prone to losing her temper, yet tolerant, Albert was more reserved, a scholarly minded man who was a stickler for morals. He really was her right-hand man, a perfect bureaucrat who enjoyed spending his hours writing ministerial minutes. The couple spent their days working side by side at their respective desks. Albert also ran the royal household and for the first time in decades managed to put the finances into the black. Perhaps the highlight of his career, however, was the Great Exhibition of 1851, held in Crystal Palace in Hyde Park, that he conceived to show off the achievements of Britain.

**THE GRIEVING WIDOW** Unfortunately Albert also put Victoria into the black on December 14, 1861 when he died. Her grief was powerful and obsessive. It also showed her left-handed proclivity for fantasy. Victoria's fantasy was a sentimental one, and it became one of the dominant flavors of the Victorian era, to be found in the poetry, for instance, of Alfred, Lord Tennyson, but more than anything else embodied in the life of the Queen herself.

Following Albert's death she ordered the preservation of his rooms in the royal homes at Balmoral Castle, Osborne on the Isle of Wight and Windsor. Every evening, Albert's clothes were laid out on his bed and a pitcher of hot water and clean towels were brought in. The routine would be maintained for the next 40 years and every night she went to her lonely bed with one of his nightshirts and a plaster cast of his arm, while a portrait of Albert hung above his side of the royal bed. Victoria herself adopted the widow's uniform of dressing in black which she would continue to wear for the remaining half of her life. When her daughter Alice was married the year after Albert's death, Victoria told her elder daughter, "it felt more like a funeral than a wedding" and that it was like "a dagger is plunged in my bleeding, desolate heart."

In the years subsequent to Albert's death Victoria engaged in a bout of serious memorializing, composing an *Album Inconsolatium* which contained condolence letters as well as poems and literary musings on the nature of life after death. She commissioned a biographer to write the story of Albert's life. For Theodore Martin, this task would take five volumes and 14 years of his life. A mausoleum costing $400,000 was built in the grounds of Windsor Castle to house Albert's body, and Victoria intended hers to join him there. A national Albert Memorial was commissioned for Hyde Park, to be paid for by the government. Ten years after his death, the Royal Albert Hall was completed. At its opening, Queen Victoria was too overcome to make her speech and her son the Prince of Wales had to step in. In cities all around the British Empire, statues, roads, schools, parks and libraries appeared to immortalize the Prince Consort. It comes as no surprise to learn that Queen Victoria employed mediums to try and make contact with Albert in the afterlife.

This grieving ultimately had a damaging effect on her monarchy. Having been a conspicuous and popular monarch up until that time, as the monuments to Albert multiplied Victoria became more and more reclusive. The initial sympathy of her subjects cooled with the feeling as the

excessive grieving went on, that their Queen had abandoned them. To some extent she had. Her grieving was fantastic in that it constituted a refusal of reality. As a child, Victoria was known for her tremendous stubbornness, and her extended mourning was evidence of this trait. Like many of the great left-handers in this book, she was prepared to go against the world in order to express her sense of singularity.

**WIDOW TO WIDOW** Although it could be argued that Victoria had abandoned her public, in private she continued with the work of her monarchy, approving the decisions of Cabinet, following shifts in power in Europe while placing her children into beneficial marriages. For much of the time, Victoria was an interested participant in Britain's affairs of state, though she no longer had the power to exercise her will independently of Parliament. While her forceful character and keen intelligence enabled her to influence political decisions, she was rarely able to make them.

On one occasion, however, she intuitively used her grief to further the harmony between Britain and the United States. On hearing that Abraham Lincoln had been assassinated Victoria, who had already been the subject of several assassination attempts herself, wrote his wife Mary a touching letter:

> Dear Madam, though I am a stranger to you, I cannot remain silent when so terrible a calamity has fallen upon you and your country, and must express personally my deep and heartfelt sympathy with you under the shocking circumstances of your present misfortune. No one can appreciate better than I can, who am myself utterly broken-hearted by the loss of my own beloved husband, who was the light of my life, my stay, my all, what your sufferings must be; and I earnestly pray that you be supported by Him to Whom alone the sorely stricken can look for comfort in this hour of heavy affliction! With the renewed expression of true sympathy, I remain, dear Madam, your sincere friend, Victoria R.

Although the letter seems a bit over the top in a contemporary context, it was nonetheless a heartfelt condolence and Mary Lincoln was very grateful. The public release of the letter also improved the reputation of Britain in its former colonies. Although Britain had initially seemed to favor the South, Victoria had declared neutrality in the Civil War. Her ability to empathize, from her own experience, with Mary Lincoln did much to erase any residual antipathy left over between the two former enemy states.

**LIBERAL QUEEN** Victoria's ability to empathize with those who were different from her was a hallmark of her reign, and a trait that left-handers often possess. It helps explain her capacity for friendship with a much older man such as Lord Melbourne. She also enjoyed a profound relationship with another prime minister, Benjamin Disraeli. Disraeli

**LEFTY LINKS**

1. Victoria's grieving for Albert was both excessive and obsessive. Obsessiveness is a trait many of the people in this book seem to share, although it's hard to know whether it might be related to handedness or is simply that people who achieve great things are likely to have obsessive personalities. Alexander the Great was certainly obsessive in his need to conquer, while Michelangelo's attempts to conquer nature through art displays a similar pathology and Ramses the Great's monument-building program showed a fanatical self-regard. Joan of Arc's adherence to her vision evidences an excessive streak in her character while Newton became so obsessed with a mathematical problem that he forgot to eat. Nietzsche was a philosophical obsessive, while Hendrix invested his obsessiveness in the guitar to the extent that he would rather starve than get a day job.

2. Although Victoria ruled over a period in British history known as the 99-year peace, she was something of a warrior queen during the small wars and skirmishes that punctuated the peace. The major military engagements were the Crimean and Boer wars, while there were a number of rebellions in Britain's colonies that necessitated military intervention. During these times, Victoria was prone to badgering her ministers to distraction. Lord Panmure, Secretary for War during the Crimean campaign, referred to Victoria's thirst for news of the war to a parched traveler in the desert's longing for water. Of course as a nineteenth-century constitutional monarch, Victoria was unable to instigate military action, but one wonders how she might have compared to other lefty conquerors such as Ramses, Alexander, Julius Caesar and Napoleon, with whom at least she shared the distinction of presiding over some of the world's greatest empires.

3. Left-handedness runs in Victoria's family. Contemporary members of the British Royal Family who are left-handed include Prince Charles and Prince William, while King George II and King George VI were also left-handed.

was the first person of Jewish descent to become Britain's Prime Minister (and the last). As a left-handed woman whose first language was German, Victoria knew what it was like to be an outsider. As the ruler of an empire which was composed of disparate peoples, this capacity to empathize with the strange came in handy, most notably when she took on the title of the Empress of India in 1877. Victoria was in many ways a proto-multiculturalist. She didn't believe all the subjects under her dominion needed to be Christian. When she met with subjects from India she enjoyed the exoticism of their native dress. She elevated one of her waiters, Abdul Karim, an Indian Muslim, into the role of one of her most intimate servants and spent many hours learning Hindi from him. He brought his family with him and they established a Muslim enclave at her court. On the other hand, she saw no reason why an educated black man couldn't become an Anglican archbishop.

**JUST DON'T CALL ME QUEEN** One prime minister who Victoria never got on with was the reformer William Gladstone. This was due to a clash of personality styles as much as disagreement over policies, such as Gladstone's fervent belief in Irish Home Rule and pacificism in matters of foreign policy. Whereas Melbourne and Disraeli appealed to the passionate spirit of Victoria and were romanticized as a consequence, she famously complained that Gladstone "speaks to me as if I were a public meeting." As an early biographer Lytton Strachey put it:

> She had no objection to being considered as an institution; she was one and she knew it. But she was a woman too, and to be considered only as an institution—that was unbearable. And thus all Mr Gladstone's zeal and devotion, his ceremonious phrases, his low bows, his punctilious correctitudes, were utterly wasted.

Here we get a sense that Victoria never completely lost the anti-authoritarian streak often found in left-handers. Even though she was the Queen, she preferred people who treated her as a person. Further evidence of this trait can be found from her choice of intimates in the second outwardly gloomy stage of her life: John Brown the high-spirited Scottish highlander who was frequently drunk and treated Victoria without any regal respect at all and the Munshi, Abdul Karim, whose role at court vexed many of her traditionalist aides.

**CODA** The Victorian era came to an end in 1901 when Victoria died at the home in the Isle of Wight that she and Albert had bought for themselves, and where she often went to escape the formal pressures of the monarchy. The period through which she reigned was the height of British greatness and although the dominant image of her in history is as a stern widow, Victoria was much more than this. A smart operator with an intuitive grasp of politics and family, her left-handed qualities made her a leader whose personality came to characterize an entire period of history.

OPPOSITE: CROWDS LINE A CENTRAL LONDON STREET TO WATCH QUEEN VICTORIA PASSING IN HER DIAMOND JUBILEE PROCESSION, JUNE 1897.

PAGE 120: QUEEN VICTORIA ON THE OCCASION OF HER 66TH BIRTHDAY.

_Lewis Carroll_

1832–98 FEW BOOKS OCCUPY SUCH A BELOVED PLACE IN THE COLLECTIVE imagination as Lewis Carroll's _Alice's Adventures in Wonderland_ and _Through the Looking Glass_. Tales of a young girl and her adventures in a nonsense world, they have fascinated adults and children alike for more than a century and are as fresh on the page today as the day they were published. The reputation of their creator is rather different. He was a shy and stammering Oxford mathematics don and Anglican clergyman, a conservative with a dull social persona who only came truly alive when writing or in the company of young girls. In this day and age, it's doubtful whether his pursuit of relationships with young girls, which included photographing them naked, would be tolerated. Even in his own era, he was clearly a square peg in a round hole, a classic case of a left-hander whose uniqueness never formed an easy fit with society. Despite being a gifted mathematician and pioneer in the field of photography, he ultimately preferred the transformational logics of his fantasy worlds, which were an imaginative and left-handed revolt against the repressive strictures of his boffinish bachelor existence. His writing has been a major influence, not just on children's literature, but on emerging literary genres, such as fantasy, as well as twentieth-century artistic movements, such as Surrealism and Absurdism.

**YOUNG LEWIS** Lewis Carroll was born Charles Dodgson in 1832 (Lewis Carroll was only ever his pen name). He was the third child and first boy in a family of 11 children, all of whom would survive until adulthood. His father was a gifted mathematician who had abandoned a promising academic career by becoming a country parson. As a child, Carroll was a comfortable and charismatic presence within his family, yet an awkward stammering child outside. It's possible that this trait may have been linked to his left-handedness, or to the attempt to make him

122

## LEWIS CARROLL'S LEFTY TRAITS

**EMPATHETIC** Carroll was able to understand how children thought and invent stories and jokes which delighted them.

**LATERAL THINKING** A master of transformational thinking, Carroll converted logic into nonsense, parodied people and society and generated sufficient absurdity to create entire fantasy worlds, whose whimsy continues to enchant adults and children alike.

**SOLITARY** Carroll is another famous left-hander whose romantic life was non-existent. He was close to his brothers and sisters, and very fond of a long line of little girls, but his emotional life never seemed to make it into the real world.

**ICONOCLASTIC** Although in life Carroll was deeply conservative, his imagination was paradoxically anarchic and afflicted with a kind of comic nihilism.

**EXPERIMENTAL** Carroll pretty much created a whole new genre of comic writing whose influence stretches from the nonsense verse of Edward Lear to the shenanigans of Britain's Monty Python and the Goons, to Douglas Adams' *Hitchhiker's Guide to the Galaxy*. Carroll also demonstrated his experimental side as a pioneer of the photographic arts.

**FANTASIST** Carroll has written what is arguably the most famous literary fantasy of all time.

Carroll was deeply ambivalent about the idea of becoming a full-time clergyman. He viewed his academic job as a stepping stone and means of financial support for his real ambitions which were primarily literary. By the end of his first full year of teaching, Carroll wrote in his diary:

> I am weary of lecturing and discouraged. It is thankless, uphill work, goading unwilling men to learning they have no taste for, to the inevitable neglect of others who really want to get on.

Still, he would remain a math lecturer for another 25 years.

Carroll had been writing creatively since a very young age. It was something of a family hobby that Carroll shared with his brothers and sisters, who swapped and competed against each other with poems whose contents were filled with the surreal violence that children love. One can almost imagine the close siblings also getting great satisfaction out of their kind of "violence" to the words—which caused them so much bother in public due to the stammering—by turning them into nonsense. The rectory in Croft was a hive of creativity with Carroll at the helm, writing and acting out plays, showing off to his sisters with conjuring tricks, perplexing them with riddles, and entreating them to contribute to editions of the family's in-house magazine. The satisfaction Carroll obtained from this period determined the way he would achieve posterity, and the unparalleled happiness he experienced with his young sisters, may be the reason he would enjoy the company of little girls for the remainder of his life.

**ALICE** During his university years, Carroll contributed to national humor magazines such as *The Comic Times* and *Train*, as well as more local publications such as *The Whitby Gazette*. He was constantly thinking of ways in which he could earn money by writing. The impetus for his great success, however, would come not from the conventional pursuit of a literary career, but from hanging out with the daughters of his effective boss, the Dean of Christ Church, Henry Liddell.

Carroll inveigled his way into friendship with the Liddell children through photography. Like many left-handers, Carroll had an experimental streak and was a pioneer photographer who bought his first camera in 1857. One day that year, he and a friend entered the Deanery garden with the intention of taking photos of Christ Church Cathedral, and ended up taking photos of the Liddell children, Harry, Lorina, Alice and Edith, instead. After this, Carroll became a frequent visitor to the Liddells, often behind Mrs Liddell's back, though it is unclear as to whether snobbery or maternal instincts were the reason for her uneven resistance to Carroll's increasing presence.

Carroll seems to have won over Mrs Liddell's confidence, however, since she allowed her children to go on boating excursions with him over several summers. During these excursions Carroll would make up stories to

_Mark Twain_

1835–1910 MARK TWAIN IS ONE OF AMERICA'S GREATEST AUTHORS, AND THE first to write books in American colloquial English. Twain was a man who cultivated experience. His restless spirit saw him lead a varied life and, in addition to being a novelist, he was also a lecturer, journalist, travel writer, miner, printer, Mississippi steamboat pilot and failed inventor. In this he was the classic left-hander, a divergent thinker and dabbler whose many experiences found value through their deployment in the subject matter of his books. The popularity of his books and his quick-witted, peppery personality endeared him to the world and, along with authors such as Charles Dickens, he was at the pinnacle of a late-nineteenth century vogue for celebrity novelists. For some time, Twain carried the reputation of being the funniest man in the world. Yet in his view, laughter was only ever a kind of compensation for its sufferings. His personal life was marred by the death of his wife and three of his four children and led to the bleak and aphoristic conclusion that "there is no laughter in heaven." However, his humor, in books such as _The Adventures of Tom Sawyer_ and _The Adventures of Huckleberry Finn_, struck powerful blows for racial equality and the commonsense of the everyman against the pretensions of "society." The iconoclastic intention of his humor was an embodiment of both the left-hander as rebel and the ethos of life in the American West. The vivid worlds he re-created in his books surge with human energy and have delighted millions of readers and continue to do so today.

**SAMUEL CLEMENS** Samuel Langhorne Clemens was born in Florida, Missouri, but he moved to Hannibal, Missouri on the western banks of the Mississippi as a small child. His father was a socially respectable, but financially disastrous, judge and Clemens' childhood was one of genteel poverty, exacerbated by his father's death, which saw

Be good & you will be lonesome.

The face of the water, in time, became a wonderful book—a book that was a dead language to the uneducated passenger, but which told its mind to me without reserve, delivering its most cherished secrets as clearly as if it uttered them with a voice. And it was not a book to be read once and thrown aside, for it had a new story to tell every day.

This job of "reading the river," which involved acute observation honed by experience and intuition, was ideally suited to Clemens' lefty temperament. He relished the aura of being a river sage and, if the Civil War hadn't intervened to close down much of the river traffic, and his younger brother, Henry, hadn't been killed in an explosion while working on a steamboat, Clemens may well have remained on the river for the rest of his life. Being a riverboat pilot certainly helped Clemens hone his observational skills, of both people and his natural surroundings. Like Leonardo da Vinci's belief in the importance of basing one's art directly on nature, Clemens believed in the priority of the senses, of the value of interpreting the real world, writing about the people he knew in the language they spoke. Clemens also derived his more famous nom de plume from this period of his life. "Mark Twain" was the call the pilots used to indicate the depth of two fathoms (12 feet), meaning the boat was safe from running aground.

After a brief interlude as a member of Confederate militia, Clemens escaped the Civil War by heading west with his older brother, Orion, who had been appointed Secretary for the Nevada Territories. He embraced the possibilities of frontier experience, including a period living in a miners' camp, in an unsuccessful attempt to find his fortune in gold at California's Jackass Hill.

Having failed as a miner, Clemens reverted to journalism and increasingly made his living by transforming his experiences into humorous pieces signed "Mark Twain," which were published in newspapers and magazines across America. His rising popularity as a humorist led to a tour to Europe, which he popularized in his second book, *Innocents Abroad*, which remains the number one selling American travel book. By this stage, those who didn't already know Samuel Clemens never would. To the world, Clemens had effectively become Mark Twain and it was Mark Twain who would mine the experiences of his former self.

So how is all this related to the fact that Twain was left-handed? One thing left-handers have been proven to be good at is adapting or transforming objects for new uses. This is not surprising, given that everyday objects and tasks, such as scissors, or writing in a notebook, can demand some form of adaptation. On a more profound level, there is also evidence to suggest that the right hemisphere of the brain is more responsible for new associations such as finding new uses for things, or navigating new places, while the left hemisphere is more involved in the maintenance of everyday associations. This might partly explain the restless hunger for

"ALL MODERN AMERICAN LITERATURE COMES FROM ONE BOOK BY MARK TWAIN CALLED *HUCKLEBERRY FINN*. AMERICAN WRITING COMES FROM THAT. THERE IS NOTHING BEFORE. THERE HAS BEEN NOTHING AS GOOD SINCE."

ERNEST HEMINGWAY

OPPOSITE: MARK TWAIN ON THE DECK OF A STEAMBOAT, 1901. IN 1857, CLEMENS BECAME AN APPRENTICE MISSISSIPPI STEAM BOAT PILOT. HIS NOM DE PLUME, "MARK TWAIN," WAS A TERM USED BY RIVERBOAT PILOTS TO MEAN "TWO FATHOMS."

## MARK TWAIN'S LEFTY TRAITS

**INTUITIVE** Twain was a powerful believer in the primacy of the naturally good heart as a way for finding one's way in the world. In his own life he followed his impulses, even if it did lead to mistakes.

**EMPATHETIC** As a writer, one of Twain's strengths was his ability to see the action from the perspective of his characters. This is one reason why *Huckleberry Finn* is a far better book about anti-slavery than other works, such as Harriet Beecher Stowe's *Uncle Tom's Cabin*, which viewed the issue as a matter of Christian morality, without letting go of racial distance. It is Huck's actual friendship with Jim that determines his moral choices.

**LATERAL THINKING** In his early life, Twain had many careers. Even when he became a wealthy author he invested in a number of madcap business schemes which eventually cost him his fortune, forcing him to embark on an around-the-world lecture tour in 1895, to rescue himself from bankruptcy. His humor is also based on surprising combinations and ironies, again an example of lateral thinking.

**HOT-TEMPERED** Twain's dry and sardonic sense of humor could be biting and his quotes and aphorisms have a decidedly peppery flavor. However, he was also prone to losing it completely for stupid reasons. For example, a visitor turned up to Twain's Hartford Connecticut house to find him throwing all of his extensive shirt collection out of a second floor window. The reason—because he had found ONE shirt where a missing button hadn't been sewn on.

**ICONOCLASTIC** Twain changed the whole direction of American literature by writing in the colloquial voice.

**SELF-TAUGHT** Twain learned by experience and throughout his life preferred this form of learning over the dry abstractions of learning in the classroom.

**EXPERIMENTAL** Twain liked to try new things. Many of his experiments in life, business and art were unsuccessful, yet this very openness was a crucial part of the way he became one of the first great American authors.

new experience in Clemens' character which is evidenced by his many careers, his travels and the multitude of places he chose to live in. It's also interesting in terms of the way that Clemens became Mark Twain. One of the striking things about most lists of famous left-handers is how many left-handed actors there are. While actors rarely change the world (hence their relatively small representation in this book), they are particularly good at changing themselves. Actors earn their living by finding new uses for themselves through their transformation into different characters. In both his non-fiction books and his novels such as *Life on the Mississippi* and *The Adventures of Tom Sawyer*, as well as his renowned performances on the lecture circuit, Twain showed a similar ability to transform himself and his experiences into richly humorous situations that were based on events from his actual life.

**HUCKLEBERRY FINN** By the time Twain wrote his masterpiece, *The Adventures of Huckleberry Finn*, in 1884, he was wealthy and living in Hartford, Connecticut. He had escaped from his boisterous frontier days to marry a frail, deeply religious and socially superior woman named Olivia Langdon. Together they had four children of whom only one, Clara, would survive her father. For the unruly boy turned riverboat pilot, turned miner, turned western humorist, it was another work of self-transformation, which included the adopting of the white suit as his everyday dress. Yet, this life change was also about setting himself up in a world where he could feel iconoclastic, as he settled down to write the majority of his books that were based on the comparatively rude joys of his former life.

*Huckleberry Finn* was a powerfully iconoclastic book. The language used in the dialog between Huck and the runaway slave, Jim—the protagonists of *Huckleberry Finn*—is not the kind of English Twain would have learned at school. Nor is it the language he would have been likely to use in the genteel environs of his Connecticut home. It is the kind of language Twain knew from his childhood and youth. Until he wrote *Huckleberry Finn* it wasn't the kind of language you'd be able to find in a book. Unsurprisingly, the book was banned from many libraries. The Concord Library in Massachusetts, home to some of America's early literary culture, banned it because it was "trashy and vicious," while the Brooklyn Public Library banned it in 1902 because it used "scratched" as well as "itched," and "sweat" instead of "perspiration." Here we can see the division between the earthy language favored by Twain and the more abstract preferences of America's literary elite, which mirrors the distinction between experiential versus schooled knowledge, seen in both *The Adventures of Tom Sawyer* and *Huckleberry Finn*. Many agreed with him. Twain wrote to his publisher that the Concord ban should sell them another 20,000 copies of the book.

Of course it's not just the language which is iconoclastic in *Huckleberry Finn*. One of the most radical things about the book is the fact that Huck, the barely schooled son of the local drunk, is the book's narrator. While such characters often appeared in books, it was extremely rare to find them telling the story directly. Throughout his book, Huck Finn has the moral dilemma of whether to turn Jim in so he is sent back to his owner, Miss Watson, or to help Jim's quest for freedom. Again, Huck is faced with a choice between the concrete and the abstract, between natural goodness versus social codes, between Jim—whom he grows to recognize as a human being—or the antebellum moral code, which the Christian religion used to justify slavery. After being puzzled by this dilemma for most of the book, Huck eventually takes the left-handed path and commits to helping Jim with the exclamation, "All right, then, I'll GO to hell." As always, Twain comes down in favor of the unorthodox informed by the natural goodness of the heart.

*Huckleberry Finn* ends with Huck saying, "But I reckon I got to light out for the Territory ahead of the rest, because Aunt Sally she's going to adopt me and civilize me, and I can't stand it. I been there before."

# Friedrich Nietzsche

**1844–1900**    ALTHOUGH LARGELY UNHERALDED IN HIS LIFETIME, NIETZSCHE HAS become one of the foremost figures in the Western philosophical tradition. He wrote his philosophy in a witty, iconoclastic style and, like a true left-handed rebel, refused the logical convenience of a philosophical system. He is primarily remembered for his notion of the "Ubermensch," or "Superman," and his philosophy of extreme individualism and self-overcoming was particularly influential in the emergence of Existentialism. His idea of the "Will to Power," which he developed from his engagement with the work of the German philosopher Arthur Schopenhauer, was misappropriated by the Nazis (Nietzsche had contempt for anti-Semitism) and was also crucial in the thinking of the French post-structuralist movement, which is the dominant philosophical fashion of today.

Nietzsche was a man with appalling health, but immense intellectual vanity—and the genius to justify it. He lived the latter part of his life on the hop, stopping at various destinations in Germany, France, Switzerland and Italy, lodging in cheap boarding houses, where he worked far beyond the limitations of his delicate health. The close circle of friends who remained devoted to him, despite his increasingly erratic behavior, were prone to talk of him in awe and pity as a man who had left society behind. Freud would describe him having "more penetrating knowledge of himself than any man who ever lived or was likely to live."

The stories of great lefties in this book are often those of people going against the tide, using their lefty uniqueness to resist the crushing forces of convention in order that their innate genius may flower. The tragic tale of Nietzsche is one of the most powerful examples. Despite an outer life that, at times, seems hardly a life at all, his philosophical texts broke radically new ground in the field and continue to be vital to our conception of the world today. His writing style, with its use of pithy aphorisms and

## NIETZSCHE'S LEFTY TRAITS

**INTUITIVE** Nietzsche worked without a philosophical system and Sigmund Freud credited him with having more knowledge of himself than anyone, something that can only be achieved through intuition rather than logic.

**HOT-TEMPERED** Nietzsche was scathing of his enemies and prone to being over-demanding of his friends and family. However most of his rage was distilled and delivered in the brilliant iconoclasm of his work which embodied the Dionysian principle. As Zarathustra said, "I love the great despisers, because they are the great adorers."

**SOLITARY** Nietzsche considered marriage, but the only time he proposed he was rebuffed. He spent huge amounts of time by himself, something that was amplified by the fact that he rarely stayed in the same place for more than a couple of months.

**ICONOCLASTIC** One of the great iconoclasts of all time, Nietzsche once wrote, "[I am] a man who wishes nothing more than daily to lose some reassuring belief, who seeks and finds his happiness in this daily greater liberation of the mind. It may be that I want to be even more of a freethinker than I can be."

**EXPERIMENTAL** The aphoristic style of philosophy that Nietzsche evolved was a revolutionary new way of writing philosophical texts. To a large extent he was also the guinea pig of his own philosophy.

of it are noticeable in lefty geniuses as diverse as Michelangelo, Beethoven and Joan of Arc, but none seems to have been possessed by the drive for individuality as strongly as Nietzsche. For this reason he has been an inspiration to legions of social rebels since, including Jean Paul Sartre, rock star Jim Morrison, author Henry Miller and Beatnik writer Jack Kerouac.

**THE BIRTH OF TRAGEDY (1872)** One of the key lefty moments in Nietzsche's philosophy was in his first book, *The Birth of Tragedy*, when he offered a radical and romantic reinterpretation of Ancient Greek and European Culture. At the time, the prevailing view in Europe was that Ancient Greece was the highlight of civilization, a society predicated upon the complementary values of rationality and serenity. Nietzsche turned this on its head by arguing that this "Apollonian" (the ancient Greek sun god) rationality, whose most conspicuous proselytizers were post-Socratic philosophers, such as Plato and Aristotle, had been preceded by a darker creative energy which Nietzsche characterized as Dionysian—after Dionysus, the ancient Greek god of wine and intoxication, also the patron of the stage. For Nietzsche, the Dionysian was an instinct-driven, wild, chaotic, amoral and natural energy that was the well-spring not just of creativity but of life itself. Against this he contrasted the Apollonian forces of rational order, peace and maintaining the status quo.

The Dionysian is the energy of the rebel, the individualist and the artist. It also speaks to the left-hander, whereas the Apollonian, with its social order and rational harmony, speaks to the right. Nietzsche was a fan of this Dionysian energy and he thought Ancient Greek civilization started to decline as soon as the Apollonian energies of order came to dominate it.

Nietzsche's interpretation of the Dionysian is classic left-handed philosophy. We can see the Dionysian principle in Beethoven, for instance, who initiated the shift from the neatness of classical music to the craggy, creative grandeur of the Romantic era. It can also be found in the angry touch-play of John McEnroe and the nomadic wine, dine and conquer lifestyle of Alexander the Great. As Dionysus was also the Greek god of the stage, it is perhaps no surprise that so many actors are left-handed. Left-handers are often to be found at the epicenter of change. Because the world never completely fits their nature, they have less investment in the status quo to begin with. Because they are used to adapting and transforming to cope with a right-handed world, left-handers have a instinctive affinity with the forces that anticipate, instigate and facilitate change. And they often also seem to have an affinity with the creative rage that is also part of the Dionysian spirit.

**SUPERMAN** Nietzsche's masterpiece, *Thus Spake Zarathustra, A Book for All and None* (1883–85), was written once he had retired from Basel and begun his life as a wanderer. It was a remarkable work illustrating

Nietzsche's left-handed brilliance at synthesizing characters, stories, imagery and philosophical style from a range of thought traditions including the Bible, pre-socratic philosophy, Zoroastrianism and Romanticism, to create a radically new philosophical movement. It is written from the perspective of Zarathustra (Zoroaster), a Persian prophet who lived in Persia about 1,000 years before the birth of Christ. Like Nietzsche, Zarathustra had trouble gaining acceptance for his philosophy and spent much of his life as a wandering thinker in self-imposed exile. The religion he founded is notable for its lack of hierarchy and the emphasis it places on individual free will. (It is not known whether Zarathustra was left- or right-handed.)

The most famous idea of *Thus Spake Zarathustra* was the concept of the Ubermensch, literally meaning "Over-man," but usually translated into English as "Superman." Nietzsche believed that human life was dominated by what he characterized as the Will to Power. Yet those who succeeded in this quest were not so much the politicians, conquerors and despots who achieved power over others, but those who managed to achieve power over themselves. Only these people, thought Nietzsche— and there was no doubt that he considered himself among them—were able to rise beyond their humanity. Zarathustra, as the unpopular prophet who eschews society to do battle with himself in the wilderness, is the epitome of the Nietzschean superman.

Arguably, Nietzsche's formulation of the Superman is a particularly lefty notion of greatness. Because the order of society is traditionally stacked against lefties, they often prefer to do battle with themselves, relishing the challenge of the Nietzschean overcoming of the self. Beethoven's deaf composing is a powerful example of self-overcoming, as were the not always successful, on-court antics of John McEnroe—a manifestation of a struggle that was not so much about the opponent, but of conquering one's own inner demons. The perfectionism of Leonardo and Michelangelo is another instance of the Superman mode of struggle. At a certain level of greatness, lefty geniuses become their only competitor. In his maturity, Beethoven knew no artistic equal, just as Alexander had no rival. However, the struggle to become a Superman is more likely to generate intensity than to end in success, something Nietzsche eventually discovered to his cost.

**THE TRAGEDY OF MADNESS** We talk today of extreme sports. Nietzsche was a man who practiced extreme thinking. A solo explorer of the mind, his philosophy was radical and is widely considered to have marked a conceptual break between the nineteenth and twentieth century. He remains one of the most vital influences in modern philosophy today. However, like many who base-jump from buildings or climb the world's highest mountains, his extremism would eventually cost him his health and sanity. Lefties seem to stand a better chance of being geniuses than righties, but they also seem to have a greater chance of being insane, particularly in

*Henry Ford*

1863–1947 IN 1888, WHEN HENRY FORD LEFT THE FAMILY FARM IN DEARBORN FOR the factories of Detroit with a head full of mechanical dreams, the ratio of America's urban to rural population was 1:4. By the time he died in 1947, it was 4:1. One of the main causes of this was that the car he invented, the Model T Ford, had extended the range of people's daily lives, making possible the kinds of cities with roads and suburbs we know today. In its years of manufacture between 1908 and 1927, the Model T, also known as the Tin Lizzie or Flivver, sold over 15 million units. It was the biggest-selling car of its time by far. At one stage during its production, more than 90 percent of the world's cars were Fords. Henry Ford is widely credited as the man who "put America on wheels." In doing so he revolutionized manufacturing by pioneering the assembly line. By 1947, one in seven American workers were employed in the automotive and related industries. Ford's novel thinking in terms of staff salaries was also a crucial factor in the expansion of the middle classes that was necessary to create a mass consumer society. Sadly, the latter part of Ford's life was a classic case of left-handed brilliance gone awry. He became a crank, and an advocate of causes such as anti-Semitism. Unable to move past his perfect moment of the Model T, Ford also resisted further innovation at his motor company. By the time he died, his paranoid, erratic and autocratic management had brought the Ford Motor Company to the brink of collapse.

**PUTTING THE CAR ON THE ROAD** Like many great lefties, Ford was a man whose thoughts were not bent into shape by too many years of formal education. As the eldest son, he was expected to take over the family farm but, like Isaac Newton, he had no interest in farm work at all. Ford saw his first self-propeled machine at the age of 10 when a steam-powered engine that was used for threshing and powering saws

GENTLEMEM OUR COUNTRY

HENRY FORD. AND HIS FIRST CAR.

was attached to a set of wheels by a drive train. The experience, said Ford, "showed me that I was by instinct an engineer." By the time he was 15, Ford had become known in the neighborhood as a watch repairman. In 1879, he left for Detroit to work as an apprentice machinist. While he returned at times to work on the farm, his heart was never in it and he was always looking for a way to escape. In 1891, Ford became an engineer with the Edison Illuminating Company, a position whose salary allowed him the luxury of funding his own inventions. His garage tinkering culminated in 1896 with his first self-propeled vehicle, a quadricycle.

Ford's subsequent attempts to start an automobile company reveal his stubbornness in pursuit of his vision, and capacity for bucking against received wisdom. While not a lefty solitary in the true sense, since he was very close to his wife, Clara, and a fond, if flawed, father to his son, Edsel, Ford was an extremely singular character. Before he gained sole control of Ford, he was involved in a number of car companies, which failed due to his singular vision and inability to share power. His first car company, the Detroit Automobile Company, went broke because Ford spent too much time in improving the design of his auto and not enough selling it. He

147

1. One of the features of lefty thinking is the tendency to think in holistic, rather than linear, terms. An effect of right-hemisphere dominance is that lefties tend to have more communication between the two hemispheres of the brain than righties do. Whereas linear thinking tends to plod along, step by step, toward a logical conclusion, holistic thinking operates more at the level of a vision, with the brain working subconsciously and intuitively across a multiplicity of connections until the solution appears in its entirety as a flash of inspiration. Examples of holistic lefty thinking can be found in the way Julius Caesar defeated Pompey in Greece, or the way Beethoven was able to break the form of classical music and permeate it with the organic logic of Romanticism.

2. Like Leonardo, Henry Ford was a vegetarian with a restless mind. From making cars to funding peace ships to running an anti-Semitic newspaper, he was a geyser of thoughts, both good and bad. In 1934 at the Chicago World Fair, the Ford exhibit featured an elaborate presentation about the potential of soybeans, including a menu of soy dishes such as celery stuffed with soybean cheese, soybean croquettes with tomato sauce, soybean bread, cocoa with soybean milk, and assorted soybean cookies. Ford was not just interested in soybeans for their food value either. By 1935, Ford used soybeans in the manufacture of window trim, accelerator pedals, door handles and paint for his automobiles. Ford even made a prototype soy car body.

PREVIOUS PAGES: HENRY FORD'S MODEL T AUTOMOBILE WAS A RESOUNDING SUCCESS, SINCE THE MODEST PRICE MEANT THAT THE AVERAGE PERSON COULD AFFORD ONE, THEREBY INCREASING SALES.

resigned from the subsequent Henry Ford Company when they brought in Henry M. Leland to run production (the company later became Cadillac). Finally, he started the Ford Motor Company in 1903, whose history is full of power struggles involving its founder. Perhaps most notable was his overbearing treatment of his only son, Edsel, the stress of which helped bring about Edsel's premature death. In his dotage, Ford completely lost his bearings and the negative consequences of his singularity affected the Ford company dramatically. Grown inflexible and viewing necessary changes as a challenge to his authority, he behaved like a classic paranoid despot, playing favorites and employing an evil henchman—former navy boxer, Harry Bennett—to run a capitalist version of the secret police within the corporation.

**THE MODEL T** Without doubt, Henry Ford's greatest achievement was the Model T Ford. The genius of Ford and the reason behind the Model T's success was a classic example of left-handed lateral thinking. Whereas other car manufacturers at the beginning of the automobile age saw things in pieces, Henry Ford's vision for the Model T was complete. His holistic vision saw that the design, production and market for the vehicle were intricately related, in a way that no one else had imagined.

The first Model T was built in 1908 and sold for the sum of $850, about one third of the price of other cars on the market at the time. Eleven thousand were sold until Ford opened a new factory in Highland Park in 1910, the first major manufacturing plant to implement the assembly line process that would revolutionize the industrial world. At his old factory it had taken 12 hours to assemble a Model T. With the new process a car could be constructed in 93 minutes.

The assembly line was the result of a change in perspective about the making of cars. The traditional approach focused on the car. Each car would occupy a space in the factory and various workers would come and work on the car in that same place until it was finished and driven away. Ford had the vision to see the bigger picture of the factory as a quasi-organic entity, through which the car passed in its various stages of production, kind of like the way blood passes through the various organs of the body. In Highland Park, the car came to the workers. An elevator took materials up to the fourth floor, where the body of the car was assembled and the upholstery fitted, before it passed down to the third floor to have its wheels and tires put on and be painted. Parts were distributed via conveyor belts, with each worker assigned a particular job. On the second floor the cars were fully assembled, then driven down a ramp past the offices on the first floor. This holistic mode of production made it eight times quicker to produce a Model T. By 1920, the factory was turning out a car a minute, and one out of every two cars in the world was a Model T.

## MAKING THE MARKET

In the early days, Henry Ford was an extremely idealistic kind of capitalist. He was a hands-on enthusiast who often expressed his loathing for the dispassionate kind of business thinking that was practiced from a distance by eastern states banks and financiers such as the Rockefellers. In Ford's mind, his factories were a direct extension of himself. When the new assembly line at Highland Park was built, with its 15,000 machines over four floors, Ford, who had a powerful lefty distaste for the bureaucratic processes of administration, spent most of his time on the factory floor where he watched and encouraged his employees as they operated the machines. Workers on the Model T were used to seeing their boss on the floor, full of energy and enigma. He would punch them playfully in the shoulder and tell them folksy and funny anecdotes while they labored under the increasing demand. When he saw a new employee struggling with his machine, he would step in and show him how to use it properly, advising him to let the machine do the work for him so he would have enough energy to go home and enjoy his family at the end of the working day. Ford workers of this era are frequently on record as saying they would have done anything for Henry Ford.

Because he was hands-on, he was in touch with the people who made and bought his automobiles. As such, he was in the position to take the approach that the success of the Model T would be massively enhanced if the kind of man making the Model T was also able to buy one. Until the Model T, owning a car was a rare and expensive business, restricted largely to the wealthy. The manufacturers were committed to the idea of the automobile as a luxury product. In the early days of the Ford Motor Company, for instance, Ford had to fight with his fellow directors in order to build the Model T in preference to larger and more exclusive vehicles.

Ford believed, as he explained to his attorney of the time, that, "The way to make automobiles is to make one automobile like another automobile, to make them all alike, to make them come through the factory just alike, just as one pin is like another pin when it comes from a pin factory." Because the Model T was a uniform product, made using the assembly line process, it was far cheaper to build. With the assembly line, the original price of $850 was reduced to $300. This dramatically increased its availability and popularity. The profits came in a flood. Ford and the other shareholders were earning more money than they knew what to do with.

At the same time as he was raking in all this money, Ford, whose unspectacular background and hands-on attitude to his factory made him capable of empathizing with his workers, noticed discontentment on the factory floor. The workers were paid $2.36 a day, which was barely enough to keep a family going. The assembly line meant that individual skills were no longer as necessary, and the faster worker had to wait for the slower ones to catch up. By 1913, for every 100 permanent worker slots, the company had to employ 1,000, as the turnover was so great. The training alone was costing over $3 million a year. One day, as he was walked through the

☞ LEFTY LINKS

3. Along with Isaac Newton, Ford defied his family's expectations that he would take over the family farm. While neither of these lefties had an interest in farming, they did benefit from a quiet rural background, which gave their minds space to think freely. Ford's later residence was a virtual wilderness retreat and he deliberately kept away from high society. Other lefties to have enjoyed the thinking space of rustic quiet include Leonardo, Beethoven and Nietzsche.

4. Ford's antipathy toward bureaucracy was typical of the intuitive lefty thinker. Once, while passing the office of a clerk and seeing his desk stacked high with paperwork, on impulse Ford picked up all the paper and stuffed it in the trash can, then told the clerk that he now had a free day. However, while intuitive and holistic approaches are great for creativity and managing small enterprises, they cause problems when organizations become so big that they need an effective administrative chain of command. Perhaps because he saw the company as an almost organic extension of himself, Ford was appalling in terms of relinquishing control. One of the problems with a lefty base of intuitive, holistic thinking is that if you lose perspective, there is no rational system to fall back on. The consequences of this are often paranoia and poor decision making. In some ways, the Model T was such a complete vision that Ford was never really able to move on from it. Despite his brilliance, after the Model T his autocratic personality, bad temper and deteriorating decision-making capacity caused a massive decline in the fortunes of the Ford Motor Company. Its survival was finally contingent upon Ford being shunted sideways by his grandson.

FOLLOWING PAGE: HENRY FORD GIVING AN ADDRESS ON NBC RADIO, C.1940. DURING WORLD WAR II FORD BECAME QUITE OUTSPOKEN ON THE SUBJECT OF ANTI-SEMITISM.

_Marie Curie_

**1867–1934**

AGAINST ALL THE ODDS, THIS BRILLIANT LEFT-HANDED POLISH WOMAN remains the only person ever to win Nobel prizes in two different scientific fields. Her prizes in Physics (1903), which she shared with her husband, Pierre, and Chemistry (1911), which she won after his death, were both related to the discovery of the radioactive element radium. In addition to a wide range of medical applications, radium was crucial for developing our understanding of how the atom is composed. This scientific understanding of the atom made possible the development of nuclear energy and weapons. Throughout her life, Marie Curie showed a powerful determination and singular focus. Unafraid to be different, she managed to break new ground in both science and society. Along with her discoveries and prizes, she was also the first female university professor in France.

**EARLY MARIE** From her early life, Marie's left-handedness was just one of the attributes which set her apart from the norm. The fact that she became a scientist at all was a victory of single-minded determination, and willingness to be different, against some serious obstacles. As a left-hander, knowing she was already different must have helped her to stick to her guns, despite the fierce social and financial obstacles that were often leveraged against her.

Marie Curie was born Maria Sklodowska, the youngest of five children in Warsaw in 1867. Her parents were of aristocratic origins but were not wealthy and struggled to make their living as teachers. At the time, Poland was split into three sections, ruled by the Russians, Prussians and Austrians respectively. Warsaw was controlled by the Russians and, following an attempted uprising in 1863, there had been a clampdown on Polish culture. Schools, for instance, were compelled to teach in Russian and, for some school children, even speaking Polish in the playground was banned. Marie's parents, patriotically Polish, rebelled against such

## MARIE CURIE'S LEFTY TRAITS

**LATERAL THINKING** Marie was innovative in her refusal to apply for patents to her discoveries and in the way she managed relations with the mining businesses who supplied her with materials. Her invention of the X-ray truck, which ran the X-ray machines using the vehicle's engine, is another example of her lateral problem solving.

**HOT-TEMPERED** Marie wore her heart on her sleeve and was prone to exploding. Her students described her as terrifying, and she never avoided a fight when she perceived an injustice was at work.

**SOLITARY** Marie sacrificed friendships for the long hours of study, and fought with her brother-in-law because he talked to her too much. In the end she found her match in a man equally fond of his solitude, who would support her single-minded devotion to science.

**ICONOCLASTIC** Marie consistently broke barriers in the quest for education. When the Nobel Prize committee urged her to refuse the Nobel Prize due to her affair with Paul Langevin, she wrote back to them to say that her scientific achievements had nothing to do with her private life.

**EXPERIMENTAL** Marie conducted experiments, then developed theories, rather than the usual scientific method of using experiments to test a pre-existing theory. She also experimented in other areas of life, such as creating among her colleagues a communal form of home schooling for their children. Her X-ray trucks are another example of the practical bent of her experimental mind.

strictures and surreptitiously helped to maintain their nation's cultural identity. At one stage her father was demoted by the Russians and the family was forced to take in student boarders in order to keep food on the table. The family's difficulties were compounded when one of these boarders brought typhoid into the house, which killed Marie's eldest sister, Zosia, in 1876. Marie's mother already had tuberculosis and, devastated by her daughter's death, she weakened and died in 1878.

Both of Marie's parents were understandably passionate about education and, unlike many left-handers, Curie was an excellent student at school. Just a few months after her mother's death, her father sent her to the Russian Gymnasium (the German name for high school), where she wasn't supposed to speak Polish at all. Despite this oppressive regime, four years later she graduated Dux in a language she didn't really like.

Once she graduated from high school, her gender made it difficult for her to continue her studies. Polish universities of the time did not admit female students and there was insufficient money in the family to fund her education in Paris. Her studies were restricted to classes taken at the illegal Flying University until she and her sister Bronia struck a deal. Marie was to work as a governess in Poland and help out her sister financially, while she studied medicine in Paris. Then when her sister had graduated, she would help support her.

After three years as a governess in the countryside, Marie returned to Warsaw and resumed classes at the Flying University while looking after her father. It was there, aged 22, that she encountered her first scientific laboratory. Until then she had been toying over whether to study literature or science but, after spending time in the laboratory, when she left for Paris a year later it was with the fixed intention of studying science.

## LIFE ON THE LEFT BANK
When Marie signed up to study science at the Sorbonne, she was one of only 23 women in a Faculty of Science that had over 1,800 students. Compared to Poland there was at least the opportunity of going to university. In Poland, however, the school of Polish Positivism, which advocated nationalism by education, was in favor of women's rights, as was shown by underground institutions such as the Flying University. In some ways sexism in France was stronger than in Poland. Most of the female students at French universities were foreign, which is not surprising given the sentiments of writers such as Octave Mirbeau, whose views that, "Woman is not a brain, she is a sex, and that is much better," were widely held.

Standing apart from the crowd was something that nurtured rather than crushed Marie. Just by being left-handed, she knew she was innately different from the vast proportion of the world. Why then should it be a problem to be Polish in France, or a woman in a world unready to acknowledge the possibility of female scientific genius? As her studies progressed, Curie became more absorbed in them. One of the consequences was a developing urge for solitude, often found in left-handed geniuses, in which she could engage with her own thoughts. First, she moved out of her sister's house, partly because her brother-in-law was too noisy. In a letter home, she wrote:

> I am working a thousand times as hard as at the beginning of my stay: in the rue d'Allemagne my little brother-in-law had the habit of disturbing me endlessly. He absolutely could not endure having me do anything but engage in agreeable chatter with him when I was home. I had to declare war on him on this subject.

It was unusual in the extreme for a female student to live by herself. Until she got married, Marie lived in a succession of small, spartan student apartments, often up five or six flights of stairs, where the water in the sink would freeze in winter. For the first year or so of study she hung out with a group of fellow Polish ex-patriot students, but again the companionship was distracting. She later remembered, "I was forced to give up these relationships, for I found that all of my energy had to be concentrated on my studies . . ."

For many people, studying in a cold apartment with little in the way of companionship would be lonely and miserable, but such was the singularity of Marie's personality and her inner compulsion that she would later remember this period of intense learning as "one of the best memories of my life, that period of solitary years exclusively devoted to the studies finally within my reach, for which I had waited so long."

The hard work was rewarded. In 1893, she took first place in the license examination for the physical sciences at the Sorbonne, roughly the equivalent of a masters degree. In July 1894, she managed second in the Sorbonne's license examination for mathematics.

**PIERRE** Marie's self-imposed solitude was interrupted, however, when she met Pierre Curie, a scientist, who was also possibly left-handed, and even more of a natural outsider than Marie. While he was already a considerable scientist he was an appalling networker who, from a combination of stubbornness and shyness, showed no inclination for playing the game. For a French male academic at the time, the career path was fairly well delin-eated: high school at one of the grandes écoles, passage to the Sorbonne or another university, a Ph.D., then a career as a professor at one of France's universities. Pierre, however, had been tutored at home, hadn't bothered to take a Ph.D.—even though he had conducted enough original research for several—and was teaching at an unfashionable school which offered him limited laboratory facilities. He lacked the superficial charm and small talk to prosper in the greasy world of academic politics. Yet his major research projects, first into the electric properties of crystals, then into magnetism, were ground-breaking.

Like Marie, Pierre craved solitude. But not completely. Within a year, the tall, dreamy-eyed 34-year-old had proposed to Marie. She in turn was

PAGE 157: MARIE CURIE WORKING IN HER LABORATORY AT THE UNIVERSITY OF PARIS, 1925.

FOLLOWING PAGES: MARIE CURIE GIVING A LECTURE TO AN AUDIENCE OF MEN AND WOMEN AT THE CONSERVATORY OF ARTS AND CRAFTS, PARIS, 1925.

powerfully drawn to this ponderous man who viewed the world with detachment, as if lost to the intense computations happening inside his head. Unlike many outsiders who dream of marrying into society, Marie felt that marrying a fellow outsider was the best way of maintaining her own autonomy. At one stage Pierre even proposed that they live in the same apartment, but in separate rooms. Torn between returning to Poland and looking after her father, and remaining in Paris and marrying, the 26-year-old Marie dithered, before finally accepting Pierre's proposal. They were married in July 1895, then set off on a bicycle tour of northern France.

**SHACKED UP AND GLOWING** While Pierre got round to organizing his papers so he could get the salary raise that came with possession of a Ph.D., Marie researched the magnetic properties of steel, ran the household, studied for a license to teach science at a girls' high school (she came first again) and became pregnant. On September 12, 1897, their first daughter, Irene, was born. Not long after giving birth, Marie began casting around for a topic for her own Ph.D.

In 1895, Wilhelm Röntgen had discovered X-rays while conducting experiments with the cathode ray tube. This launched a wave of experiments in order to ascertain the nature and application of a variety of energy rays. When Henri Becquerel, a physics professor at Paris' prestigious École Polytechnique, placed uranium salts on top of photographic plates wrapped in black paper, and put them out in the sun, he was hoping that the energy of the sun might cause the salts to emit X-rays, which would then show up on the photographic plates. The first results were positive, and he decided to repeat the experiment, adding a copper cross between the black paper and the salts, hoping its pattern would appear on the plates. This time the sun refused to shine. After some days Becquerel became impatient and developed the plates anyway. He was amazed to find they clearly showed the outline of the salts. He put the result down to a kind of invisible phosphorescence. In other words, the salts seemed to be emitting their own energetic rays.

Becquerel presented his results, but they were far less sexy than X-rays, and no one paid much attention. Except for Marie Curie. She found that the theories based around cathode ray tubes were inadequate to account for this phenomenon, and determined to discover the source of the mysterious phosphorescence that had appeared on Becquerel's plates. She begged and borrowed mineral samples from whoever would give them to her, and set up her lab in a dark, dusty shed provided by Pierre's boss. Using a small, coal-powered stove to refine the samples, and a piezoelectric quartz electrometer (invented by Pierre during his work on crystals) to measure their electric output, Marie began the quest which would lead to the discovery of radium.

Like many left-handers, who are known to prefer the concrete to the abstract, Marie took a practical approach to her work. She was always more an

OPPOSITE: MARIE AND HER HUSBAND, PIERRE, C.1904. TOGETHER THE COUPLE WOULD DISCOVER TWO NEW ELEMENTS: RADIUM AND POLONIUM.

experimental, rather than a theoretical, scientist. As such, she was a perfectionist in the laboratory. As one of her research associates later described her:

> The series of operations involved in opening the apparatus, pushing down the chronometer, lifting the weight, etc. as the piezoelectric method requires, is accomplished by Madame Curie with a discipline and perfect harmony of movements. No pianist could accomplish with greater virtuosity what the hands of Madame Curie accomplish in this special kind of work. It is a perfect technique which tends to reduce the coefficient of personal error to zero.

The raw material Marie mainly used was a mineral called pitchblende, known to contain uranium. Using the piezoelectric method, she determined that pitchblende made the air around it more conductive than pure uranium. The chances were that another radioactive element was at work. Pierre put aside his work on magnetism and began to help Marie with her research. On July 20, 1898, Marie announced the discovery of a new element called polonium, named after her homeland. By December 1898, their research revealed another element, which they called radium, since initial reckoning showed it to be 900 times more radioactive than uranium. Eventually they would demonstrate that it was 1 million times as radioactive.

Not only had Marie hit the chemist's Holy Grail of discovering not one, but two, new elements, her research had shown that radioactivity was the property of the atom. It was a crucial step in the transition from the stable matter of the Newtonian universe to the unstable atomic world of quantum mechanics.

As an experimental and hands-on scientist, Marie didn't put her energy into pursuing these changes to the theory of the universe. Both polonium and radium existed only as trace elements in pitchblende and Marie spent most of the next three years perfecting her technique for distilling tiny quantities of these elements from the raw material, while wondering what radium would look like when enough of it was accumulated to give it physical presence.

**NUCLEAR FISSION** In 1903, Marie and Pierre were given half of the Nobel Prize for Physics, shared with Henri Becquerel. Yet the discrimination because she was a woman remained. Despite the fact it was Marie who had made the actual discovery, the prize would have been given to Pierre only if wasn't for his insistence that she share in it. When Pierre was appointed Professor at the Sorbonne the year after, social convention usurped their scientific equality and Marie was appointed as his assistant. Still, the chance to leave the shed for a spec-built laboratory and be paid to work together overcame any irritation at the discrimination. The year 1904 also saw the birth of their second daughter, Eve.

Tragedy struck in 1906 when the absent-minded Pierre was crushed to death by a carriage loaded with six tons of goods. Marie was devastated and retreated into her laboratory. Ironically Pierre's death was good for her career. Marie was appointed Assistant Professor at the Sorbonne, the first female professor in France.

One person Marie became close to was the physicist Paul Langevin, who had been good friends with Pierre. He was in an unhappy marriage and the two of them became intimate. By 1907, this intimacy had developed into a full-blooded affair. In 1911, just as the Swedish Academy was deciding to give Marie her second Nobel Prize (for Chemistry), the scandal of their affair became public. From being considered a French heroine, Marie was then perceived as a Pole whose scientific abilities paled before her theft of the husband of a French woman. The situation worsened when extracts from their love letters were leaked and published in the press.

Spooked by the publicity, the Nobel Prize Committee wrote to ask Marie to refuse the prize until the true accusations of her adultery had been proven false. Again, Marie showed a left-hander's capacity to stand up to social convention, writing back to them, "The action which you appear to advise would be a grave error on my part. In fact the prize has been awarded for the discovery of Radium and Polonium. I believe there is no connection between my scientific work and the facts of private life." Deciding to accept her second Nobel Prize means that, even today, Marie Curie is the only person in its history to win Nobel prizes in separate disciplines. She is also one of only four women to win the prize in the hard sciences. Of the other three, one is her left-handed daughter, Irene Joliot-Curie, who won the Chemistry prize in 1935, together with her husband Frederic, for their work on the synthesis of radioactive elements.

**LATER LIFE** Most of Marie's breakthroughs were achieved while Pierre was still alive. The rest of her career was primarily devoted to accumulating radium and creating the scientific infrastructure to explore its usefulness. Her other achievements include the foundation of the Radium Institute. During World War I, she observed the need for X-ray facilities at the front. Although horses still outnumbered vehicles, she realized that X-ray machines could be powered by motor vehicle engines, so she established a fleet of X-ray trucks to go out to the military hospitals. They carried out over a million wartime examinations with the result that many limbs and lives were saved. Similarly, she mounted two campaigns in America to raise money to buy grams of radium: one to further the Radium Institute's research, the second to set up Poland's first nuclear medicine facility. She was also appointed to the League of Nations Committee on International Co-operation.

Marie's experiments with radium weakened her health over a long period of time, and her latter years were marked by illness. In the end she died of aplastic anemia brought about by exposure to radiation. Yet through her left-handed capacity to be different and stay different, she was able to overcome myriad social and economic hurdles to become one the greatest scientists the world has known.

 LEFTY LINKS

1. Not only was Marie Curie left-handed, but photographic evidence suggests it is likely that both Pierre and daughter Irene were also left-handed. This is particularly interesting since Irene also went on to win a Nobel Prize for her work with her husband, Frederic Joliot-Curie who, judging by the way he holds his cigarette in photos, may also have been left-handed.

2. Something Curie shared in common with her fellow left-handed scientist Isaac Newton, was a tendency to get so absorbed in her work that she frequently forgot to eat. At one stage she became so weak that she fainted and was forced to confess to her brother-in-law, Kazimierz, that she had only eaten radishes and cherries in the preceding 24 hours.

3. Marie Curie like many left-handers, demonstrated a preference for the experimental over the theoretical; the concrete over the abstract. This inclination is also found in the writing of Mark Twain, in Leonardo's belief in the primacy of the eye and nature, and even in Nietzsche's aversion to philosophical systems.

## GANDHI'S LEFTY TRAITS

**INTUITIVE** Gandhi was a great intuitive thinker who not only had ingenious and unexpected answers to political problems, but a powerful grasp of political timing to maximize the impact of his actions.

**EMPATHETIC** Although Gandhi could be a tyrant in his ascetic demands on his followers, he was revered as *bapu* (father) to India's people. His empathy was fueled by his Jainist philosophy of non-violence to living things.

**LATERAL THINKING** Gandhi was quite brilliant in this arena. How many people could turn a long walk in search of a pinch of salt into a fully fledged independence movement?

**HOT-TEMPERED** As a child Gandhi was known for his temper, which followed him into his youth. As an adult, however, he sought to control this with spiritual discipline.

**SOLITARY** Gandhi was not really solitary, but he was celibate. He also tried to keep every Monday as a day of silence and meditation, during which, if forced to communicate, he did so in writing.

**ICONOCLASTIC** Gandhi used the British tradition against itself and, while remaining a devout Hindu, did much to break down some of its traditional inequalities.

**SELF-TAUGHT** Gandhi read few books and gained his wisdom from action and having the humility to learn from his mistakes.

**EXPERIMENTAL** Gandhi described his life as a series of "Experiments with Truth." Rather than scientific experiments, Gandhi conducted tests on how to live and how to get one's way against powerful opposition when one had moral right.

**FANTASIST** Gandhi believed in a rustic India that was never really possible, but his dream was beautiful and inspiring nonetheless.

form this involves wearing a face mask to protect bugs from death by inhalation and the refusal to eat root vegetables because it means killing the whole plant. The powerful influence of his mother's beliefs meant that, throughout his life, Gandhi was a non-drinking vegetarian who fasted for spiritual benefit, and believed in asceticism and the energy to be gained from the sublimation of sensual urges. Gandhi's father died when he was 16. At the precise moment of his death, Gandhi had been having sex with his wife, Kasturbai—whom he had married when he was 13—and the coincidence germinated an abhorrence for the sexual act. In his adult life, he would prove his powers of lateral thinking by incorporating these spiritual influences of his childhood into a mode of political action.

The young Gandhi, however, showed little sign of his impending greatness. He was a poor student and one of the reasons may well have been because he was forced to write with his right hand. Left-handedness was strongly stigmatized in India. One reason for this was that Indians traditionally eat with their hands. As such, the right hand is used for food, the left for ablutions. While left-handers can swap hands, it is often viewed with suspicion. Furthermore, in some Hindu religious practices, the right hand is sacrosanct and the left hand banned. Taboos exist, for instance, against the use of the left hand for *pooja* (worship ritual) and *prasad* (holy food). In some areas (especially rural), a marriage can be rejected if the bride or, less commonly, the groom, is left-handed. This can lead to harassment since wives are not allowed to use the left hand for cooking or serving. To ensure this, the hand can be branded, burned or hit to discourage its use. Children are also dissuaded and prevented from using their left hands for writing, eating and many daily activities. Upon showing a preference, their left hands might also be hit or have chili powder rubbed into them, be tied behind their backs or put in a bag. Some photos show Gandhi writing with his right hand and this is probably why. Interestingly, he never developed a love of reading or of writing, despite becoming a lawyer.

When he finished school his parents sent him to England. It was an act of desperation. He had only just graduated from high school in India and his grades weren't good enough to guarantee entry into an Indian university, let alone pass once he got there. On the other hand, the exams to join the bar at London's Inner Temple, as much a guild as an educational establishment, were reputed to be so easy that even a dunderhead son like Gandhi should be able to pass.

**ENGLISH LESSONS** Gandhi arrived in England in 1888 at the age of 18. Somewhat comically, he tried to use his lefty facility for adaptation to turn himself into the complete Englishman. He bought a morning suit, a top hat and a silver-headed cane. He purchased a violin and embarked on a range of "civilizing" classes—violin, elocution, dancing and French. He learned the hit songs of the time and accompanied young women to dances without informing them that he was already married.

All this aping of the English ended, however, when Gandhi ran out of money. Unable to eat the mutton dishes served up by his landlady, he was extremely happy when he came across a vegetarian restaurant while walking around London. Inside the restaurant was a book by the anarchistic thinker H. S. Salt titled *A Plea for Vegetarianism*. As he read this book a bell went off in his brain. It provided reasons, through rational argument, for what had been dictated to him by custom, myth and religion. With his frivolous pursuits behind him, Gandhi was inspired. He joined the Vegetarian Society. More importantly, he began a series of dietary exercises based on Salt's book, which became the first of what he called his "Experiments with Truth," whereby he would measure the effect of adopting a discipline on his spiritual well-being.

Some of the Vegetarian Society members also belonged to the Theosophy movement, which believed that every religion contained a portion of the absolute truth, a belief compatible with Gandhi's Pranami heritage. As Gandhi moved in these circles, he was introduced to a variety of literature. Importantly, he began to become acquainted with Indian culture via British scholarship. Although he knew Hinduism intimately from direct experience, the first time he read its holy text, the *Bhagavad Gita*, was in English translated by Edwin Arnold from the ancient Sanskrit. Through his access to these ancient texts, Gandhi came to form a picture of his ideal India; one that was spiritual yet different from the image perpetuated by the Brahmins, who had arrogated knowledge of the Hindu scriptures into a self-serving system of hereditary caste. Gandhi learned about the Buddha through Arnold's long poem, *The Light of Asia*, read the Bible and was deeply influenced by the New Testament—while abhorring the Old. He also learned about Mahomet via English writers such as Thomas Carlyle. It was the most significant reading period of Gandhi's life. In later life, preferring reality to theory, he was never a big reader and these texts, with the addition of works by Tolstoy and Ruskin, were the bedrock of his literary influence.

At the same time that he was absorbing these books, Gandhi was also learning the practical tradition of the English Common Law with its organic system of precedent, whereby judgments in former cases came to constitute the law. Having abandoned his attempts to emulate the English, and probably without really knowing it, he was intuitively positioning himself to become a hybrid of traditional Indian and progressive English liberal values, perfectly placed to take on the British, on their own terms, while simultaneously appealing to his fellow Indians.

## BOERISH SOCIETY

When Gandhi completed his studies in 1891, he returned to India. It wasn't a happy time. His mother had died and the family's influence at the court in Porbander had waned. He tried to set up as a barrister in Bombay, but made a laughing stock of himself when he was struck dumb with stage fright when presenting his first case. In 1885, a Muslim trading house in Porbander asked him to travel to

PAGE 167: MOHANDAS KARAMCHAND GANDHI WAS GIVEN THE NAME *MAHATMA*, MEANING "GREAT SOUL" BY NOBEL PRIZE-WINNING BENGALI POET, TAGORE, FOLLOWING HIS TRIUMPH OVER THE BRITISH AT CHAMPARAN.

face of the Indian's non-violent resistance. This caused a public outcry against the government by the white people it was pertaining to represent. Gandhi believed that it was important to the possibility of peace that people be able to relinquish their positions without losing face. Smuts was eventually forced to negotiate with Gandhi and a compromise was reached, even if its conditions would be eroded after Gandhi had returned to India.

**HOME RULE** When Gandhi returned to India in 1915, he set up an ashram devoted to truth, non-violence (*ahimsa*), celibacy, vegetarianism, non-materialism and serving the Indian people. It was a strict and ascetic outfit, over which Gandhi ruled somewhat tyrannically.

It wasn't long, however, before he became involved with India's Congress Party and with campaigns that used *satyagraha* to fight injustice. Gandhi's first success came while advocating the interests of the indigo farmers of Champaran near the border of Nepal. The price of indigo had collapsed due to the invention of aniline dyes. As a result, the mainly British landowners began charging their tenant farmers cash on top of the indigo they supplied, reducing the farmers to a state of desperate poverty. The farmers had been protesting this through local lawyers, who claimed their fees, but had thus far failed to deliver a result. Gandhi entered the region of dispute and convinced the lawyers to become his assistants. Soon after, the police ordered him to leave because his presence was considered a danger to public peace. He refused and was brought before the courts, where he pleaded guilty. Instead of being sent to prison, the charges were dropped. An enquiry ensued which resulted in the landowners being forced to compensate the farmers.

At Champaran, Gandhi had stood up to the British and won. For this he was given the title *mahatma* (meaning "Great Soul") by Nobel prize-winning Bengali poet, Tagore. It also made him a hero across India. His next campaign was within the Indian community: leading a strike against a mill-owner over wages. After two weeks of strike, the boss wasn't budging and, faced with hungry families, the workers began to weaken. Seeing this, Gandhi had an intuitive brainwave. He announced that he would go on a hunger strike if the strikers relinquished their claim. It was the first time he had used this strategy and it worked. Not only did the strikers keep going, but faced with this new resolve the mill-owner gave in.

Following the 1919 Amritsar massacre, in which British troops fired on an unarmed Indian crowd, killing at least 400 with thousands more casualties, Gandhi's attitude began to harden toward the English, while still opposing the violence advocated by other members of the Indian resistance. His policy of non-cooperation encouraged people to boycott British products and wear *khadi*, an Indian cloth which everyone could make at home. He also urged that people should resign from government employment and boycott British institutions—schools, universities, the law courts and the system of honors. The catchword was *swaraj*, meaning full independence, not just political but spiritual and individual too.

# Charlie Chaplin

CHARLIE CHAPLIN'S LITTLE TRAMP IS ONE OF THE MOST ENDURING characters in cinema. Dapper and indigent, the "eternal non-conformist," as one critic described him, is a classic left-hander at odds with a right-handed world which always seems to be putting its dangers in front of him.

For his creator, this downtrodden everyman brought enormous power and wealth, granting Chaplin the means to try and erase the scars of an unhappy childhood and rise to the pinnacle of society. From a childhood in the slums of London, with a mentally troubled single mother forced to prostitute herself to make ends meet, at the height of his fame Chaplin was probably the most famous man in the world. Like many of his friends, he was able to build himself a fantasy life, remote from the social conventions that most of his audience lived by. The impoverished protagonist of his wonderful silent films made possible an improbable lifestyle of mansions, swimming pools, tennis courts and liaisons with a vast array of stunningly beautiful women. In many ways, Chaplin's life was a kind of human alchemy, perhaps one of the most resonant examples of the left-hander's facility for transformation.

**UPBRINGING** Chaplin was the second son of music hall entertainers, who separated when he was three. His father was a ballad singer, while his mother, who had gypsy heritage, sang and played the piano. Charlie Chaplin Snr. was a committed alcoholic who rarely saw his son, except for a brief period when Charlie and his half-brother Sydney lived with him and his mistress. He died from alcohol-related cirrhosis of the liver when Charlie was only 12. Life for Charlie and Sydney was tough, living with their mother, who lost her singing voice, and whose straight acting skills weren't sufficient to provide a living. They all lived in unsalubrious lodgings, ate sparingly and, like many in the theater, Hannah Chaplin turned at times to prostitution to make ends meet when roles were not

of compensation: for the insecurity of his childhood and the, not always, happy creativity that ruled his temperament.

The waning of Chaplin's creative powers saw him enter the final great relationship of his life. At the age of 54 he married 18-year-old Oona O'Neill, daughter of American playwright Eugene O'Neill (who never spoke to his daughter again after her marriage). It proved an enduring and loving, if not entirely happy, marriage, and they had eight children together.

**LATER LIFE** All through his career, Chaplin showed a studied indifference for social conventions and got away with it. He put risqué material into his comedy that contraverted the ill-policed Hollywood code of conduct, and he slept with innumerable teenage starlets. While he was one of the wealthiest figures in Hollywood, he also became known as a communist sympathizer, and began associating conspicuously with the cream of the artistic and intellectual left. As someone whose life trajectory had proven so preposterously against the odds, he continued to ride them, carefully managing his cinema output to challenge the status quo but not so much that he'd be shut down.

Of course the period between the wars was known first for the decadence of the 1920s and then the Depression of the 1930s and, in some ways, Chaplin's political views followed the zeitgeist. When World War II broke out, he contributed by lampooning Hitler, who had at one time been a tramp—and who had in fact modeled his mustache on the Little Tramp's in the belief that it would enhance his popularity. *The Great Dictator* (1940) caused some consternation as the USA was yet to enter the war.

After the war Chaplin hit a snag by underestimating the aggressive paranoia of the McCarthy era. Attacks on Chaplin had been growing in the USA since the end of the war. He was particularly vulnerable to government sanction since he had never become an American citizen. In 1952, when he left for the English premier of *Limelight*, he learned that his re-entry permit would not be renewed. Chaplin was forced to settle instead in Switzerland, where he remained for the rest of his life. Soon after this, he embarked on a film, *A King in New York*. Shot on London sets made to resemble New York, it was the first film to directly criticize the paranoia of the McCarthy era. While it received warm criticism in London, it wouldn't be shown in America for 15 years.

**CURTAINS** Chaplin only made one more feature film after that, *The Countess from Hong Kong* (1967), a flop starring Marlon Brando and Sophia Loren. Chaplin and Brando had a major clash of egos and the film only covered its production costs because one of the songs Chaplin had written became a hit for British pop star Petula Clark. In the last 20 years of his life, Chaplin wrote a number of autobiographical books which rather gilded the lily. He died in his sleep in 1977 only to become a prop in a real life comedy when Polish and Bulgarian mechanics stole his body and hid it in the hope of selling it back to the family.

 **LEFTY LINKS**

1. It seems there are a disproportionate number of left-handers in the pantheon of successful actors. A possible reason is that lefties naturally developthe facility for adaptation and self-transformation, integral to their engagement with a right-handed world. In some cases it has helped the kind of body awareness necessary for mimicry. Three of the great mimics of the twentieth century—Chaplin, Marcel Marceau and W. C. Fields—were all left-handers. Other famous left-handed actors include Don Adams, Dan Aykroyd, Matthew Broderick, Drew Carey, Tom Cruise, Matt Dillon, Olivia de Havilland, Robert DeNiro, Fran Drescher, Richard Dreyfuss, Peter Fonda, Greta Garbo, Whoopie Goldberg, Betty Grable, Cary Grant, Mark Hamill, Rex Harrison, Goldie Hawn, Rock Hudson, Angelina Jolie, Danny Kaye, Diane Keaton, Nicole Kidman, Lisa Kudrow, Michael Landon, Hope Lange, Joey Lawrence, Peter Lawford, Shirley MacLaine, Harpo Marx, Marilyn Monroe, Kim Novak, Ryan O'Neal, Sarah Jessica Parker, Anthony Perkins, Luke Perry, Richard Pryor, Ronald Reagan, Robert Redford, Keanu Reeves, Julia Roberts, Mickey Rourke, Telly Savalas, Jerry Seinfeld, Christian Slater, Terence Stamp, Rod Steiger, Emma Thompson, Peter Ustinov, Dick Van Dyke and Bruce Willis.

2. One of the things about left-handers is their facility for adaptation and change, which may be why they can be found excelling in the Protean moments of history. Chaplin prospered at the beginning of the film era because an orthodox way of doing things was yet to be established. The same might be said for Jimi Hendrix, Paul McCartney and music, Henry Ford and the automobile industry, as well as Bill Gates in computers. Having less invested in the status quo, the lefty has an innate capacity to seize the moment of change. As the philosopher Walter Benjamin once said, "all the decisive blows are struck left-handed."

3. Chaplin's left-handedness probably came from his mother. Spencer Dryden, who was the son of Charlie's half-brother Wheeler Dryden (same mother, different father), was the drummer in Jefferson Airplane and was also left-handed.

never really went for books or writing. His literacy wasn't helped by being forced to write with his right hand, and his sentiments toward school were in line with the famous boys in the tales of lefty author Mark Twain. Today, Ruth would have been diagnosed with attention deficit hyperactivity disorder (ADHD) and dosed with Ritalin. Ruth was a natural rebel and the strictures and emotional shortfalls of his boyhood meant there was something coiled up inside his spirit that was busting to be unleashed. He may well have turned to crime, were it not for baseball.

A terrible place to spend a childhood in many ways, St. Mary's had the singular advantage of being an excellent place to shine on the baseball diamond—except for the fact they had no right-handed mitts for lefty fielders. Academic studies were not taken too seriously and the Xaverian Brothers were often young men from poor families who had joined the church because it offered three square meals a day. Many of them were young enough to still be playing baseball. With so many boys around, it was always possible to put together a team. As a result, Ruth played baseball every day, 10 months a year. Since his parents never visited on Sundays, he played baseball. Since he never got to go home for holidays, he played it too. And well. Brother Matthias, 6 foot 6 inches and a good batter of both boys and balls, noticed Ruth's talent and encouraged it. The school had its own baseball league, which borrowed the names of major teams, and played each other. Ruth became the school's star pitcher and hitter. He became a hero to his fellow residents, a status he would retain for the rest of his life.

**STARTING OUT** On February 14, 1914, acting on information from a brother coaching a baseball team from a competition Xaverian Brothers school, Jack Dunn, owner and manager of the minor league Baltimore Orioles, went down to St. Mary's to take a look at Ruth and came back having signed him as a left-handed pitcher for $250 a month. For Ruth it was an unfathomable amount of money. At Spring training in Fayetteville, North Carolina, where he rode in a train and elevator for the first time in his life, he acquired his nickname and hit the longest home run the local ground had ever seen.

After Ruth's first season pitching for the Orioles, Dunn had financial problems and sold him to the major league Boston Red Sox. Ruth didn't want to leave his friends but he took the raise ($625 a month)—and the train. He showed his lefty impulsiveness by picking up the 16-year-old waitress in the Back Bay station diner he breakfasted in when he got off the train. She would later become his wife. He then went to Fenway Park, home of the Red Sox, and was fitted for a uniform before playing that afternoon and pitching his first seven innings in major league baseball for a win.

In a game where those who reach the top echelons usually have been playing since they were young, a left-handed pitch forces a batter to adapt his pre-conditioned responses. In other words, a left-hander's pitches take a few micro-seconds to adjust to, but only if they remain in the minority. This is a pure example of the left-hander's enhanced capacity to surprise an

OPPOSITE: AS A PITCHER, "THE BABE" WAS FORCED TO WEAR A RIGHT-HANDED GLOVE AS LEFTY GLOVES WERE NOT YET AVAILABLE.

PAGE 187: KNOWN AS THE "SULTAN OF SWAT" AND THE "COLOSSUS OF CLOUT," RUTH PLAYED FOR THE YANKEES FROM 1920–34.

## ALAN TURING'S LEFTY TRAITS

**INTUITIVE** Turing's mathematical method was brilliantly intuitive and he often came to conclusions without relying on prior research in the field.

**VISUAL-SPATIAL ABILITY** This was seen in Turing's ability to visualize concrete solutions to abstract mathematical problems.

**LATERAL THINKING** Similar to the above, Turing had the mental ability to transform the abstract into the concrete and vice versa.

**SOLITARY** As a mathematician, Turing was famous for solving problems on his own and, with the exception of his boyhood friend Christopher, his emotional life remained solitary, even if he was capable of being a convivial companion.

**ICONOCLASTIC** Turing was unashamed of his homosexuality, and the creative anarchy of his Bletchley Park days demonstrated his contempt for mindless authority.

**SELF-TAUGHT** Turing taught himself to read in three weeks at the age of five, and many of his adult ideas sprung from the way science books had affected his imagination as a child. Never one for the formalities of the classroom, he achieved his mathematical breakthroughs with an unusual degree of independence from the thoughts of others.

**EXPERIMENTAL** From an early age Turing loved to perform chemical experiments, and his interest in engineering the actual technology that proved his mathematical conclusions, showed that there was an empirical side to this mathematical genius.

all accounts phenomenally messy as a child. Around 1924, he discovered chemistry and was attracted by the simplicity of the way atoms were put together. Yet being a child of the English upper middle classes, chemistry was viewed by his parents as a sideline of the main game, which was a public school education, with the requisite emphasis upon the classics. Rescued from the deeply conservative Marlborough College by his older brother's observation that it would squash him, Turing was sent to the slightly less repressive Sherbourne College. In this nonetheless highly conformist environment, Turing was soon conspicuous as a friendless solitary. His mind was already committed to math and science and his report cards noted his lack of effort in the subjects he wasn't interested in. Even in math, his masters were ambivalent. While his teacher was sufficiently amazed at his ability to solve complex equations to remark that he was a genius, he also wrote on his report card, "Not very good. He spends a good deal of time apparently in investigations in advanced mathematics to the neglect of elementary work. A solid groundwork is essential in any subject. His work is dirty." His form master in 1927, A. H. Trelawny Ross, believed that Germany's defeat in World War II was due to the fact that Germany "thought that science and materialism were stronger than religious thought and observance." A teacher of English and Latin, he was fond of saying, "This room smells of mathematics! Go out and fetch a disinfectant spray." Such a mediocre education had little effect on Turing, other than to consolidate the independence of his left-handed mind. It gave him the impression that thinking was a solitary activity practiced by relatively few, and learning was a thing you did by yourself. Ignoring his lessons, he spent his time instead reading and "improving" upon Einstein's Theory of Relativity.

Turing's isolation was breached that same year, when he fell in love with Christopher Morcom, a small and slight boy a year older than him. Socially awkward and incapable of small talk, Turing was able to form a bond with Christopher through their shared fascination with science. They applied for Trinity scholarships together, and Turing was disappointed when Christopher got one and he didn't. He was even more devastated soon after when, in February 1930, Christopher was admitted to hospital with complications from childhood bovine tuberculosis and died six days after. His only real friend was gone.

**CAMBRIDGE** The death of Christopher proved to be a motivation in Turing's subsequent mathematical career for a number of reasons. In his grief he determined that he would continue his scientific career on behalf of Christopher as well. His innate facility and fascination with science now had a powerful emotional underpinning.

The following year, Turing won a scholarship to his second-choice college at Cambridge, King's. It was serendipitous. A small college with a tolerance both of eccentricity and homosexuality and some excellent scientists, it was an ideal place for Turing's unique talents to prosper.

In 1935, Turing was elected a Fellow of King's College with the backing of the great economist, John Maynard Keynes. It provided a stipend, rooms, High Table dining privileges and no duties, and was the perfect job for a lefty individualist such as Turing.

Christopher's death also provoked Turing to existential musings. One of the mathematical expressions of this, which displayed his capacity for lateral thought, was his engagement with the decision problem. The decision problem asks whether the human faculty of reasoning can be reduced to computation. The seventeenth-century German mathematician, Gottfried Leibniz (famous for inventing calculus independently of Isaac Newton and also for the binary number system on which computers are based), had envisioned a calculus of reason, whereby debates between men could be solved by calculation. Turing's approach to the problem showed striking originality. He invented an idealized machine which consisted of a tape divided into squares (like toilet paper) over which a scanner passes writing and/or erasing a succession of binary zeros and ones. Such a simple machine was able to do all sorts of complicated mathematical calculations. It became known as a "Turing machine." A particular feature of the Turing machine was that each machine's function could be encapsulated in a single number which could be fed into another machine. What this meant is that when a machine was fed the number of another machine it would imitate its functions perfectly. This became known as a "universal Turing machine" and was the precursor to the digital computers in use today. In answer to the decision question, Turing concluded that in certain cases, such as when a machine was fed its own number and worked on itself, there would be insoluble logical conundrums, similar to the paradox "I am lying." Leibniz's dream of a calculus of reason was proven impossible, yet the computer age had been born. Its progenitor, Turing, was only 23 years old.

Just as he was putting the finishing touches to his work on the decision problem, Turing discovered it had also been solved by a Princeton University mathematician Alonzo Church using a technique called lambda calculus. Even though Turing's solution was more elegant, he decided to take a Ph.D. at Princeton under Church. He graduated in 1938 and returned to Cambridge, where he argued with Wittgenstein over math and philosophy. One of their major bones of contention was that Wittgenstein believed that no one had ever been hurt by a logical contradiction. Turing had shown by his machines that he considered the abstract in concrete ways. It's a propensity often found in left-handers, one he shared for instance with Marie Curie, whose experiments preceded theory. As a mathematician this wasn't so easy to do, though Turing passionately believed that mathematics had an effect on the real world. He replied to Wittgenstein that a logical contradiction in an equation used to design a bridge might cause it to fall down. However, the true, real world value of his mathematical genius was about to be manifested in a far more dramatic context.

PAGE 195: CODE-BREAKER ALAN TURING PICTURED IN 1952, DURING THE TIME HE WAS WORKING AT MANCHESTER UNIVERSITY IN ENGLAND.

While Turing's left-handed brilliance was saving the British war effort, it was not particularly simpatico with army life. An eccentric figure, Turing had a strong affinity with reason and was relatively immune to social convention. When faced with the problem of hayfever while riding his bicycle to work, he simply wore a gas mask. At Bletchley, his leadership of Hut 8, according to his biographer, Andrew Hodges, resulted in an environment of "creative anarchy." This radical, left-handed individualism didn't necessarily mesh well with the bureaucracy. As his colleague of the time Peter Hilton claimed:

> His procedure . . . would be maybe to come in at midday and work until midnight the next day. And then, the problem essentially solved, go off and rest up and not come back for 24 hours perhaps . . . they were getting much more work out of Alan Turing that way. But, as I say, the bureaucrats came along and wanted forms to be filled in and wanted us to clock in, and so on.

More vital was the fact that, due to turf wars in the services, there was always a problem of staffing at Bletchley. Many in the Armed Services hierarchy didn't want to credit breaking the Enigma codes with their true importance, because it meant losing some of their authority to make decisions. The idea of a bunch of ill-disciplined boffins controlling the war effort appalled them. Turing was impatient with fools and failed to deal very well in a world where petty ego, rather than reason, could be responsible for decision making. The situation with staffing became so serious that, in the end, Turing went over the heads of everyone to British Prime Minister, Winston Churchill. The Prime Minister, who was the only official with direct access to all the decoded Enigma messages, ordered that the Bletchley mob be given whatever they needed as a matter of "extreme priority."

**POST WAR TURING** After the war, Turing contributed to various pioneering computer projects before settling down at Manchester University, where he was the director of the computing laboratory that produced the world's first commercially available computer. But for most of the twilight of his career, Turing's attention branched off into an area which, ultimately, would be related to theories of handedness. Turing became interested in the mathematics of biological structures—such as why, for instance, the heads of broccoli are congruent with the Fibonacci series. His particular interest was on how asymmetry can arise out of symmetric conditions. His answer, a brilliant piece of intuitive scientific thinking, was that a possible cause was the non-linearity of chemical equations of reaction and diffusion. The calculations to test this idea were simply too many to be able to be done by hand but, because he had access to a computer, it was possible for him to test model chemical reactions. It was a founding moment in the kinds of non-linear dynamic theory, that now include Chaos Theory and the complex modeling of financial markets.

Turing's willingness to be different and his indifference to social norms brought him undone in 1952. One day while walking in Manchester he caught the eye of a 19-year-old, working-class youth called Arnold Murray. It became something of a rough trade affair. However, when Turing was invited to appear on the BBC radio debate on the issue "Can Automatic Calculating Machines Be Said to Think," his lover tipped off a mate, who robbed Turing's house while he was out. Because he was a homosexual, the burglars didn't expect Turing would go to the police, for fear of being outed. Turing, however, did. It was an unwise thing to have done. In the course of explaining to the police who he thought was responsible, he admitted to the affair with Arnold, and gave the police no option but to charge him with gross indecency—the offense Oscar Wilde had been charged with in 1885.

Turing was sentenced to two years' probation and a course of estrogen therapy, a form of chemical castration. On the surface his life seemed far from shattered. The case hadn't received widespread media attention and, after the effects of the hormone therapy wore off, he traveled to Greece for a romantic liaison. Yet other events were troubling. For a long time after the war, Turing had continued to work for British intelligence. With his conviction, he lost his security clearance, since homosexuals were particularly vulnerable to blackmail. He also became disenchanted with a society that he had done so much to help. In some ways it was a crisis of faith. Turing sought solutions outside of science, immersing himself in the literature of Tolstoy, and having sessions with a Jungian therapist. While there is at least a conspiracy theory case for his assassination, it seems more likely that when he ate the apple laced with cyanide on June 7, 1954, it was a successful suicide attempt.

THE ENIGMA MACHINE, USED BY THE GERMANS DURING WORLD WAR II TO SEND CODED MESSAGES.

_Jimi Hendrix_ (signature)

FEW PEOPLE HAVE DEFINED THE WAY A MUSICAL INSTRUMENT IS USED TO the extent that Jimi Hendrix did. Rated by _Rolling Stone_ magazine as the greatest guitarist of all time, the combination of his unorthodox left-handed playing, embrace of fledgling electronic sound technologies and obsessive pursuit of his own unique vision, massively expanded the instrument's sonic possibilities. From a poverty-stricken childhood and grueling musical apprenticeship, Hendrix emerged to become one of the mega-stars of the sixties, the first African-American rock star to cross over to a predominantly white audience with his mixed race intercontinental band, the Jimi Hendrix Experience. In becoming a rock god, Hendrix took the blues and transformed it into a psychedelic experience that was accompanied by outrageous fashion, major-league drug taking, and a stage act that matched the wildness of the music with stunts such as playing the guitar with his teeth, smashing guitars and setting them on fire.

**EARLY LIFE** Jimi Hendrix was born into a poor but multi-racial district of Seattle, Washington. He was the cause of his parents', Lucille and Al's, shotgun marriage. Knowing he was about to be drafted into World War II, Al Hendrix accelerated his courtship of the 16-year-old Lucille with the consequence that she fell pregnant with Jimi. Al then went off to war. Jimi would be three years old and already in foster care before he met his father.

Lucille and Al were both big drinkers and not very good at holding down jobs. They fought and broke up on a regular basis and the Hendrix children were frequently shuffled around in a range of official and unofficial foster care arrangements. Genetically, they were not a great match. While Jimi and his brother, Leon, were healthy, their younger siblings were not so lucky: Joe was born with two rows of teeth, a club foot and a cleft palate; Kathy was born blind; Pamela had health problems and died

## LEFTY LINKS

1. Hendrix is far from being the only great left-handed guitarist. Other influential left-handed players include Duane Allman of the sixties band the Allman Brothers, who *Rolling Stone* voted in 2003 as the second best guitarist ever (behind Hendrix). Other left-handed guitarists in *Rolling Stone*'s Top 100 include Nirvana's Kurt Cobain (12); blues guitarist and Dylan sideman Mike Bloomfield (22); Dire Straits virtuoso Mark Knopfler (27); surf guitar pioneer Dick Dale (31); King Crimson's Robert Fripp (42); "the world's greatest unknown guitarist," Danny Gatton (63); blues rock legend Johnny Winter (72) and Black Sabbath axman Tony Iommi (86). One who should be on this list but isn't is blues guitarist Albert King, whose influential, string-bending guitar style resulted from the fact that he was left-handed and taught himself how to play a right-handed guitar upside down by pulling the strings down. Other left-handed guitarists include country artist Lefty Frizell; current Deep Purple guitarist Steve Morse; blues rocker Gary Moore; Smashing Pumpkins' Billy Corgan; and Noel Gallagher of Britpop band Oasis.

2. There's a theory that naturally left-handed children who are forced to use, and in particularly write with, their right hands often develop a stammer. This theory would seem to be supported in the case of Hendrix. His stammer was perhaps one reason why Hendrix was extremely underconfident about his singing in his later music career. Even once he'd become a mega-star he still didn't like to sing and, because he was a perfectionist, the recording of his vocals on his studio albums could take an excruciating amount of time. If his father hadn't tried to make him write "right," there's a chance the world would have been left with a greater legacy as a result of Hendrix being less self-conscious about the way he sang, and thus less resistant to putting his voice onto tape in the studio. The shyness and vulnerability in Hendrix's singing which resulted from this lack of verbal confidence was, however, also part of its unique charm. Another famous left-hander who had a stammer is Lewis Carroll.

young; while Alfred had developmental disabilities. The four younger children would spend little, if any, time with their parents and Al refused to admit to the paternity of all of them except Jimi and Leon.

When Jimi's parents finally broke up for good, his mother's lifestyle degenerated into full-blown alcoholism and quasi-prostitution. For most of his childhood Hendrix lived with his father. Al Hendrix was one of those classically hypocritical parents who were strict (often violently) with their kids, while pursuing a wild life of his own. Perhaps as a consequence, Jimi developed into a mostly passive rebel, although he was hyper-competitive as a musician and prone to uncontrollable rages when he had too much to drink.

**FIRST GUITARS** Hendrix was fascinated by guitars long before he had one. As a kid, one of Hendrix's favorite movies was *Johnny Guitar* (1954), a western where the hero rode into the sunset with a guitar instead of a rifle strapped to his back. According to father Al Hendrix, he would order Jimi to clean his room only to return to find him playing the broom with strands of straw scattered all over the floor. His first guitar was a battered one-string acoustic another kid had thrown out. Although his father would castigate him for spending too much time playing music, he also bought Jimi his first real guitars, a $5 right-hand acoustic guitar, then a white Super Ozark electric. When he could afford to put strings on these, he played the guitar obsessively—with the strings on upside down. Although he didn't know why, playing guitar right-handed felt instinctively wrong. Left-handed guitars were rarer and more expensive and Jimi had to make do with what he had, so he swapped the strings around, so that the low E string remained on the top and the high strings on the bottom when he played the guitar left-handed.

As with many of the great lefties of history, Hendrix's lack of formal education was perhaps a crucial factor in the development of his unique talent. A daydreaming child, he was forced to write with his right-hand by his school and father. His grades got worse and worse as he skipped school just to wander around the neighborhood or play guitar. From a B and C grade student in elementary school, he deteriorated to the point where he had to repeat ninth grade. His father blamed it on his guitar playing and Jimi often had to hide his guitar at friends' houses in case his father would get mad and smash it up. When his friends turned up at Hendrix's house with instruments, Al would shout at them that playing music wasn't going to get them a job. After repeating ninth grade, Jimi pretty much stopped going to class altogether, and just spent his time traveling round the neighborhood jamming with all the local musicians, watching and learning by imitation. By this time, his first band, the Velvetones, had played their first professional gigs, but Jimi still couldn't afford to buy himself and his first girlfriend, Betty Jean, a hamburger when they went on a date.

When Jimi began to play the electric guitar, this changed the sound because the strings were located in a different position from the pick-ups that carried the sound to the amplifier. As a result, the low strings were bright and the high strings mellow. Most of the time Hendrix played a Fender Stratocaster. Playing it upside down also made it easier for him to access the tone/volume knobs and tremolo bar, which were intrinsic to the originality of his sound.

Hendrix never learned to read or write music. He used his ear in the same way Leonardo used his eye. His constant playing and jamming trained his ear by exposing him to a variety of influences. Although he absorbed the sounds of other guitarists easily, he developed an idiosyncratic style which he would remain true to, no matter what the cost. When later serving his apprenticeship as a sideman for musicians such as Little Richard, Ike and Tina Turner and Sam Cooke, for example, he was often fired for his inability to temper his flamboyant guitar style and flashy solos. One of the reasons for his uniqueness, was that Hendrix couldn't learn by pure imitation. Instead, he had to watch how a right-handed player did something and then work out how to do it left-handed. This extra move of translating right into left, and the improvizations that inevitably permeated the process, were a big factor in the originality that, by the time he was 23 years old, would be blowing people away, including world famous guitarists such as Paul McCartney and Eric Clapton.

## FROM ARMY DAZE TO PURPLE HAZE

After dropping out of school, Hendrix was unable to support himself as a musician. Following arrests in relation to stolen vehicles, he traded in prison time for the army.

As with many a lefty legend, Hendrix proved incapable of toeing the line when it came to authority. He soon became known as a slack soldier and was eventually discharged. His discharge papers said the "Recommendation is being submitted because the individual is unable to conform to military rules and regulations. Misses bedcheck; sleeps while supposed to be working; unsatisfactory duty performance. Requires excessive supervision at all times. Was caught masturbating by members of platoon."

An even more telling insight into his attitude toward life was the observation by one of his superior officers that "Pvt Hendrix plays a musical instrument during his off-duty hours or so he says. This is one of his faults, because his mind apparently cannot function while performing duties and thinking about his guitar." Hendrix was so single-minded about his guitar playing that it left him with an attitude of dreamy diffidence toward pretty much everything else. He was a left-handed fantasist and this became increasingly pronounced when the rock 'n' roll lifestyle, with its attendant drug consumption, diminished his engagement with the realities of everyday life. Still, if Hendrix hadn't been such a bad soldier, it's likely his life would have taken a very different turn. Instead of adulation, Marshall stacks, LSD and girls, he might have been deployed

LEFTY LINKS

3. One of the key features of Hendrix's personality was his single-minded devotion toward the guitar. Because of this, he was frequently out of touch with the world. However, when it came to matters of music, he was ruthless, competitive, a perfectionist and, especially as his drug intake increased, prone to rage and paranoia. These personality traits—with the exception of the drug taking (and the women)—resemble those of Isaac Newton.

4. Both Jimi Hendrix's parents were big drinkers and Jimi inherited some of the same proclivities. Put bluntly, he was something of a drug pig. LSD, marijuana, heroin, cocaine, speed, alcohol, downers and uppers were all part of a heavily self-medicated existence. Dr. Stanley Coren has shown in his book *The Left-Hander Syndrome* that lefties are more likely to be dyslexic, schizophrenic, substance abusers and die early. His theory is that left-handedness is caused by damage sustained in the womb. It's an interesting theory in the case of the Hendrix family, with its one genius and many genetic misfirings. Unfortunately Hendrix helped the early death argument by choking on his own vomit after taking an accidental overdose of sleeping pills. Some of the other lefties in this book who died an early death include Alexander, Joan of Arc and Raphael. Other left-handed musicians who died young include Kurt Cobain, Mike Bloomfield and blues harmonica great Paul Butterfield. It's been mooted that being a left-hander in a right-handed world is more dangerous, particularly when using machinery. Or perhaps it's a potential side effect of lefty rage. However, not everyone is convinced of the early death statistics for lefties. Other reasons for righties seemingly living longer is that older lefties are more likely to have been forced to become righties, so there are less of them. Another reason is that women tend to live longer than men, and are less likely to be lefties. Many of the left-handers in this book have lived to a ripe old age.

HENDRIX TRULY EMBRACED THE
ROCK 'N' ROLL LIFESTYLE, BECOMING
ALMOST OBSESSIVE ABOUT BOTH HIS
HAIR AND CLOTHES.

PREVIOUS PAGES: HENDRIX
CLAIMED THAT HE PLAYED
'COLORS', RATHER THAN NOTES,
AND THAT HE SAW THE MUSIC IN
HIS HEAD WHILE HE PLAYED.

PAGE 203: THE YOUNG HENDRIX
PLAYED A RIGHT-HANDED GUITAR
UPSIDE DOWN, SWAPPING THE
POSITION OF THE STRINGS

to fight out the Cold War in the jungles of Vietnam—a fate that fell to many of his childhood friends. His innate left-handed inability to conform may well have saved his life (for a while at least).

After leaving the army, Hendrix formed the King Kasuals with army buddy and bassist Billy Cox, who would later play with him in the Band of Gypsys and at Woodstock. For the next three years, Hendrix scraped together a living playing the Chitlin' Circuit (African-American venues in the eastern and southern states of the USA), with his own band and, increasingly, as a sideman for bigger acts. It was a hard life. Most musicians resorted at times to day jobs to keep themselves alive. But Hendrix was far too singular: "People would say if you don't get a job you'll just starve to death. But I didn't want to take a job outside music. I tried a few jobs, including car delivery, but I always quit after a week or so." Slowly he began to build a reputation, but it didn't stop him from going hungry most of the time and being forced to rely on the kindness of women for food, accommodation and other favors.

## JIMI HENDRIX'S LEFTY TRAITS

Hendrix's real break came in 1966 when he befriended Keith Richard's girlfriend, Linda Keith, who championed his playing to a number of influential figures in the industry. He was introduced to Chas Chandler (former bass player from the Animals, turned manager), who took him to London, where he blew away the local guitar talent and had his first hits. It's as if there was no place for him in the often conservative, heavily hierarchical and racially circumscribed, music scene of early sixties USA, and it took the high and hedonistic individualism of Carnaby Street era London to find an audience where he could fully express his gift.

Another benefit of going to London, was a number of fortunate encounters which helped define his sound. Playing the right-handed guitar left-handed gave Hendrix an edge of difference compared to most other guitarists. It also set him on a path of constant innovation which would change the whole way electric guitar was played. When he first arrived in England he jammed on-stage with the Brian Auger Trinity, whose guitarist, Vic Briggs, was using an early Marshall amplifier. Briggs had never turned the amp above five. When Hendrix plugged in he turned the amp on full bore, with his guitar down, and proceeded to dazzle the audience with the wall of feedback and distortion from the Marshall. Along with The Who and Cream, Hendrix pioneered the use of the Marshall stack and the process of increasing sound volume by daisy-chaining amplifiers. Even more important was his ability to innovate using a variety of effects. When he arrived in England, Hendrix became close with electronics whizz Roger Mayer, inventor of the Octavia and Fuzz Face pedals. They distorted the sound and helped thicken the notes. Combined with his reversed stringing and Marshall these effects were crucial to the creation of his heavy, driving psychedelic sound. For a time in 1967, Mayer worked exclusively with Hendrix and their sonic explorations are the basis for many of the guitar sounds being used today. Hendrix was also the first guitarist to fully harness the potential of the wah-wah pedal. Hendrix's originality with the guitar was a classic case of the lefty adapting objects to suit his unique purposes, something every lefty learns by living in a righty world.

Hendrix's first album *Are You Experienced* was released in 1967 and was only prevented from reaching number one in Britain by the simultaneous release of the Beatles' *Sgt. Pepper's Lonely Hearts Club Band*, which featured another lefty musical genius, Paul McCartney. Hendrix now entered the rock stratosphere, with success as a crossover artist in the United States, appealing to both the white, black and, increasingly, the multi-racial hip market. By the time he played Woodstock in August 1969, Hendrix was its number one drawcard and one of the biggest rock stars in the world.

Being a rock god, however, took its toll on Hendrix, who never really knew how to say no. Little more than a year later, on September 18, 1970, the greatest left-handed guitarist who ever lived was found dead in his London apartment from an overdose of pills and alcohol. He was only 27 years old.

**INTUITIVE** With the exception of classical musicians who play to sheet music, most musicians have to be able to improvise. This demands considerable intuitive ability since they need to anticipate the moves of musicians they are playing with. Hendrix, as a sideman, then as a bandleader, was good at this. He also absorbed other guitar players' styles.

**EMPATHY** Particular evidence of this faculty can be seen by the fact that, wherever Hendrix went, he always found women who helped him and championed his cause.

**HOT-TEMPERED** Hendrix was prone to violent, drunken rages. He once beat his girlfriend, Kathy Etchingham, in a London pub with a public telephone because he thought she was calling another man. On another occasion he threw a vodka bottle that smashed when it hit her in the head. In 1968 he was arrested for trashing a Stockholm hotel room after a night on the sauce.

**ICONOCLASTIC** Hendrix lived in an era where rebellion seemed to be the norm, but he still was largely responsible for making the electric guitar a unique instrument rather than merely an electrified acoustic guitar. The amazing distorted version of *Stars and Stripes*, which he played at Woodstock, became the anthem of his generation.

**SELF-TAUGHT** Hendrix studied by ear and observation and never learned to read or write music.

**EXPERIMENTAL** Hendrix was known particularly for his experiments with pedals and new sounds for the guitar. He was also a perfectionist and innovator in the studio, where he was at the cutting edge of recording techniques such as stereophonic sound. In his later career he tuned his guitar a semitone down to the unusual key of E flat, which further enhnaced the originality of his sound.

**FANTASIST** Always keen on escapism, often with good reason, this tendency in Hendrix was magnified by a rock 'n' roll lifestyle, with its constant touring, girls, booze and drugs.

# Bill Gates

1955–

WHEN I LEFT COLLEGE IN 1985 I HAD NEVER TOUCHED A COMPUTER. Twenty years later, life without software such as Microsoft Windows, Word, Excel and Hotmail is pretty much unimaginable. The products created by Bill Gates have arguably had a greater influence on the developed world in that time than any other. They have changed the way business is done, the way people communicate, the way creativity finds its form and culture is disseminated. Although these inventions don't necessarily belong to Gates, he was the first to see the importance of software as opposed to hardware and has operated, for the most part, with uncanny prescience in bundling these technologies into commercially savvy packages. As a consequence of this, Gates has become the richest man in the world, possibly even the richest man in history. Having made billions changing the way we live, he has now become the world's most generous philanthropist, giving back billions to help raise the standard of living through health and education programs for the underprivileged in both the developing and developed world. It's a story of a man who serendipitously landed in a moment and used his left-handed talents to make the most of it.

**CHILDHOOD** Bill Gates was born in Seattle, Washington, to a wealthy established family. His great-grandfather had been a state legislator and mayor, his grandfather the vice-president of a national bank, and his father a leading attorney, while his mother was a teacher from a socially prestigious family who served on the boards of charitable institutions and a bank. Gates was the middle of three children, the other two girls. From an early age he was intellectually curious and highly competitive. At elementary school, he outstripped his classmates in almost every subject, but showed the special affinity for math and sciences many great left-handers have had.

While an eighth-grade student at the prestigious Lakeside school, a group of mothers decided to invest the proceeds from the school's annual

**INTUITIVE** Gates' remarkable intuitive understanding of how the market for personal computers would develop, along with immaculate timing, are significant reasons for the success of Microsoft and its products.

**LATERAL THINKING** Gates is notable for his ability to contextualize technology within a business environment. In his career, he has also shown remarkable flexibility of thought. He evolved when it became clear how vital the Internet was going to become, and also had the wisdom to relinquish control of his corporation. Unlike Henry Ford, he hasn't become fixed in his thinking.

**HOT-TEMPERED** Gates' aggressive business strategies have often been accused of lacking ethics. He also established an aggressive internal culture in Microsoft, predicated on creative tension and wedded to the quality of ideas.

**SOLITARY** As an adolescent Gates became obsessed with the solitary activity of computer programming. A classic nerd, he lacked social skills and led an uneventful romantic life until he married at the relatively late age of 39.

**ICONOCLASTIC** Gates' belief that software should be sold, not shared, offended the idealist atmosphere that pervaded the nascent industry. He has also stood up to governments and has been prepared to defend these beliefs. The Microsoft culture, while competitive, has also been one in which ideas have been preferred to hierarchy.

**SELF-TAUGHT** Gates taught himself how to write the programming code that was the foundation of his immense wealth.

OPPOSITE: GATES GIVING AN ADDRESS AT THE "FUTURE FOCUS" CONFERENCE IN COPENHAGEN, DENMARK, 2001.

were shared. Microsoft's BASIC for the Altair proved very popular with computer enthusiasts, yet it wasn't long before a pre-market copy of the program was being copied and distributed for free. Gates wrote an open letter scathing of the practice, arguing that companies couldn't afford to produce high-quality software if they weren't paid. This approach earned them the ire of the community, but Gates wasn't fazed. Whether or not he was in the right, he had the successful left-hander's ability to stand up to convention and be unapologetically different in the face of considerable enmity.

Gates' approach really paid off when IBM began to look for an operating system for its new personal computers. When the first company Gates suggested to IBM couldn't come up with an agreement, IBM asked Microsoft to come up with an operating system themselves. Rather than make one, as they had for the Altair, Gates chose to licence software made by another company, Seattle Computer Products. Somewhat ruthlessly, he neglected to tell the company that IBM was the customer. Because of this, he got the software—nicknamed QDOS (Quick and Dirty Operating System)—for a far cheaper price than if Seattle Computer Products had known.

Of course, it's one thing to deceive a small company, another entirely to stand up to a corporate monolith. Gates showed even greater business acumen at the other end of the deal by refusing to sign the source code for MS-DOS (as QDOS became known) over to IBM. Consequently, when other companies started to produce clones of the IBM personal computer, Gates was in the position to licence his operating system to them as well. In contrast, his main competitor at the time, Apple, who were different from IBM in that they also made computers, refused to licence its operating system to other manufacturers, preferring to restrict itself to providing an integrated hardware and software package. As the market for PCs exploded, Microsoft products could be found not just on IBMs but Compaqs, Dells, Gateways, Hewlett Packards, Sonys and Toshibas.

One of the reasons why all these companies took up the MS-DOS software was that the licencing fee Microsoft charged wasn't too high. Following his conviction that the future lay in software, Gates had the foresight to see that providing an operating system was only the beginning of the kinds of software Microsoft would be able to sell to the buyers of PCs. By supplying the operating system cheaply, Microsoft would be in a position to make MS-DOS-compatible software for a whole range of uses such as word processing, accounting, databases and games.

**WINDOWS** The strengths of Microsoft have been to innovate and adapt. These traits are often found in left-handers who are forced from an early age to adapt to a world that hasn't been designed for them. Under Bill Gates, Microsoft has often taken ideas already in existence and adapted them to create some of its most enduring products. Perhaps the most obvious example of this is Microsoft Windows, which first appeared on the market in 1985. While early PCs ran on DOS, Apple had jumped the gun by

introducing a graphical user interface (GUI) which made its Macintosh computers much easier to use, especially for the general consumer. In order to counter this, Microsoft introduced Windows. At first it was an inferior product that survived only because there was no direct DOS-based competition. It wasn't until version 3.1 was released in 1990 that it really began to take off. It sold over 2 million copies in its first six months.

As Windows improved, it made it easier for people to use other Microsoft software, such as Word, instead of competitors' products like Word Perfect. Microsoft's domination of the personal computer was in full swing. By 1993, Windows had become the most widely used GUI operating system in the world. By 2004, it was estimated that over 90 percent of the world's PCs were running on Windows. For people who weren't interested in computers, only what they could do with them, Windows and its bundled application suites such as Microsoft Office have proved highly attractive. When you buy a PC today, it comes with a version of Windows pre-installed, meaning that Microsoft is perhaps the only company to be making money on the sale of every PC. These days, even if people want to use alternative software, such as Adobe Photoshop, unless they own a Mac or are an OpenSource geek using Linux, they are likely to do it via Windows. From the lie Bill Gates told the makers of the Altair, Microsoft has achieved astonishing penetration of the market. It has extended its share through constant innovation within its main product lines, generating new demand as the market has become more saturated through a combination of improved functionality and built-in obsolescence.

**THE CONQUEROR IN THE GATES** The business philosophy of Microsoft has been described as "embrace, extend, extinguish." They take ideas from the opposition, improve upon them, then eradicate the competition. Under Gates, who was known for his extreme competitiveness even as a child, Microsoft has pursued market share with a ruthlessness worthy of great left-handed conquerors such as Alexander, Caesar and Napoleon (in fact Judge Penfield would characterize Gates as a Napoleon during the 1998 United States versus Microsoft trial).

Business, while often being in love with the language of war, usually plays its battles out in different contexts. Microsoft has been involved in numerous court battles over the years, primarily as defendant, in a series of cases where competitors have alleged the company has abused its monopoly power. Perhaps the most famous example were the browser wars between Netscape and Microsoft in the 1990s. One of Gates' mistakes was that he was slow to recognize the dawning significance of e-mail and the Internet. Until 1995, Windows had no integrated software that could connect it to the Internet. The market leader was Netscape, who had launched their browser the year before. Netscape remained the market leader as the early versions of Microsoft Internet Explorer (IE) were inferior. However, Gates, having realized his mistake, ordered that every product Microsoft made had to be compatible with the Internet. His ability to turn the focus of such a large organization around so quickly had almost the same effect as the surprise tactics of Alexander the Great in battle over 2,000 years earlier. Successive editions of IE came to match Netscape's Navigator, feature for feature, with the advantage that the platform was more stable. Even better, for the consumer at least, IE was bundled with Windows. Netscape was effectively screwed.

In 1998, the US government sued Microsoft under anti-trust legislation which had been passed to deal with the robber barons from the end of the nineteenth century. At issue was the fact that computer manufacturers were unable to install Windows 95 without Internet Explorer. If they thought Netscape was the superior product then the best they could do was to provide a PC with both. Yet what was the point of selling a PC with two browsers? As a consequence, Netscape was losing market share drastically. When the judge ordered Microsoft to separate IE from Windows, Gates claimed it couldn't be done. He provided an older, inferior version of Windows 95 for those who didn't want to take the version bundled with IE.

**GENEROUS GATES** Although the initial judgment went against them, in the end Microsoft was able to defuse the problem, which was threatening to split them into two companies—one to manufacture the Windows Operating System, and another to provide software to work in the Windows environment in competition with other companies.

For Gates, Microsoft's anti-trust problems, which were also replicated in Europe, marked a watershed. In the middle of the case he announced his intention to stand down as CEO and hand the reins over to his Harvard friend Steve Ballmer. Gates might have perceived that his unbridled aggression presented an image problem for the company. Instead, he became chief software architect and chairman. In 2006, Gates announced his further intention to move out of a day-to-day role with Microsoft.

Unlike many of the left-handed conquerors in this book, or fellow business mogul Henry Ford, it seems Gates is unusual in knowing when to stop. Perhaps the major reason for Gates' moving on is the Bill and Melinda Gates Foundation, which began in 2000 with assets of $106 million. Since then it has expanded to possess an endowment of over $30 billion, which will only grow, since investor Warren Buffet has pledged a further $30 billion worth of shares in Berkshire Hathaway. When Gates leaves Microsoft it will be to work with the Foundation.

A mark of many of the left-handed geniuses in this book is their ability to think laterally while under the grip of an obsession. Yet many of them have eventually floundered. Gates' conversion, at such an early age, from being being a young nerd with a talent of binary code, to one of the most ruthless businessmen in the game, to one of the world's greatest ever philanthropists is perhaps an indication that in his life choices he has proved more agile than most.

1. Although it never became his career, Gates is the latest in a long line of lefties whose genius is marked to some extent by mathematical ability. Leonardo, Isaac Newton, Marie Curie, Lewis Carroll and Alan Turing are the other lefties in these pages whose genius has sprung from an innate ability at math.

2. Bill Gates shares the conqueror mentality with lefties such as Alexander the Great, Caesar and Napoleon. An argument can be made that the intrinsic apartness of left-handers enables them to be ruthless, yet without too strongly perverting their own nature. Unlike many right-handed conquerors, these lefty figures are remembered as much for what they added to the world as what they destroyed in the pursuit of their ambitions. The other great left-hander in this book, with whom Gates shares some similarity, is Henry Ford. Like Gates, Ford created the market for the Model T at the same time as he created the product. Although both men were technology boffins, they had brilliant insight into what the average person wanted from his or her products.

3. Other famous lefties that have emerged from the northwest coast of the United States include Jimi Hendrix—like Bill Gates, also from Seattle—Kurt Cobain, who was born 87 miles outside Seattle, and Matt Groening, founder of TV show *The Simpsons*, who hails from Portland, Oregon and went to school in Washington State.

# *Navratilova and McEnroe*

**MARTINA NAVRATILOVA** Tennis is a sport where the left-hander has had disproportionate success. There are several reasons for this. In a game where reaction time is measured in milliseconds, and muscle memory and rally patterns are crucial, right-handed opponents are never quite as comfortable with left-handers. Since there are less lefties, the angles they use and the spin they put on the ball are more difficult to read than those deployed by right-handers. According to some tennis experts, the fact that the left-hander's forehand serve is to the right-hander's backhand also confers an advantage. The left-hander's forehand is also the side of the court in which games are usually decided. In a game of spin and angles, it's also easy to see how the superior visual-spatial skills found in left-handed artists, military leaders and some scientists might be a factor in a game where the ball has to be hit over a net into an extremely limited space. Whatever the reasons, the evidence for left-handed tennis success is weighty: Laver, Roche, Connors, McEnroe, Nadal, Navratilova and Seles to name just a few. However, with the advent of improved racquet technology, and the growing importance of physical strength in the game, the artistry of the left-handed tennis player has recently been in decline. But in the 1980s, when tennis was riding a crest of popularity, left-handers were the best in the game.

The career of Martina Navratilova is one of those instances of a left-hander who thrives on being different. Renowned *Sports Illustrated* journalist, Frank Deford, summed it up when he wrote, "How gratifying it must have been for her to have achieved so much, triumphed so magnificently, yet always to have been the other, the odd one, alone: lefthander in a righthanded universe, gay in a straight world; defector, immigrant; the (last?) gallant volleyer among all those duplicate baseline bytes." The overweight, teenage Czech defector, who molded herself into a tennis force whose 58 combined singles and doubles Grand Slam titles (the last of them acquired at 49) are the second highest ever, is one of the great stories of modern sport.

NAVRATILOVA RECEIVING THE
WIMBLEDON LADIES SINGLES
TROPHY FROM THE DUCHESS
OF KENT, ENGLAND, 1978.

1. Left-handed male players have accounted for more than their fair share of winners over the last 50 years or so at the US Open, the French Open, the Australian Open and Wimbledon. They won 41 of the 200 singles titles at these events over the period from 1955–2004. Left-handers accounted for 15 of the winners of the men's singles titles at the US Open from 1955–2004 (30 percent of the total) and 11 at Wimbledon (22 percent). For an astonishing period of 11 consecutive years, from 1974–84, the winners of the US Open men's singles title were left-handed. As the game changed post-McEnroe, however, the lefty approach to the game suffered as tennis, with its ever bigger racquets, became more of a slugfest, played by people who spent as much time lifting weights in the gym as they did playing shots on the court. McEnroe was the last of the great touch players.

2. The list of great left-handed tennis players is a long one. Lefty men who have won Grand Slam titles include: Norman Brooks, Rod Laver, Neale Fraser, Tony Roche, Jimmy Connors, John McEnroe, Guillermo Vilas, Manuel Orantes, Roscoe Tanner, Thomas Muster, Goran Ivanisevic, Petr Korda and Rafael Nadal. Lefty women include Navratilova, Ann Haydon Jones and Monica Seles.

3. We've all heard of left-handers being forced to write right-handed. It happened to tennis players too. Australian champion Ken Rosewall, who won 10 singles Grand Slam titles, was a natural left-hander whose father taught him to play right. As a consequence he was known for his excellent backhand and suffered from a weak serve. Margaret Court, who won 24 singles Grand Slam titles and was only the second women's player to win a Grand Slam in a calendar year, also suffered from a weak serve for the same reason. She remarked in

an interview on American Cable TV that, "I wrote with my left hand, and it was at a time when people were being taught to work with their right hand; some of the male players would say that no women played left-handed. So I thought it was probably wrong to play left-handed, and I changed to right. I always think I would've had a better serve if I had been lefty." American 1950s Maureen "Little Mo" Connolly was another who was coached to swap hands. More recently, Kimiko Date, one of Japan's most successful female tennis players, was a left-hander who played right-handed because her father forced her to. One wonders how these players might have done if they'd been allowed to preserve their natural advantage.

4. As an emerging tennis player, McEnroe's hero was Rod Laver, the Australian left-hander who is the only player in Open history ever to have won two Grand Slams

(1962 and 1969), a figure all the more impressive because no male player has won the Grand Slam since. In his autobiography, *Serious*, McEnroe had this to say about Laver: "Laver was the first guy I saw who did everything – hit topspin and slice on both forehand and backhand, serve with different spins. He utilized every possible shot, all the angles. I used to have a poster of him on the back of my bedroom door. The fact that he was a lefty like me was a big deal, and that massive Popeye forearm of his just seemed so cool."

Similarly Navratilova remembers that when she heard that Rod Laver had described her as a player to watch, "she lived off that compliment . . . If Rod Laver thought I was going to be good I figured I better be."

5. What happens then when left-handers play other left-handers? While McEnroe's hero was a lefty, partly chosen because he was a lefty, he

didn't necessarily get on with all lefties. In the same autobiography, McEnroe talks about the difficult relationship he had with Jimmy Connors and how they used to trash-talk each other while changing ends when they played against each other. It's a rivalry perhaps reminiscent of the animosity Michelangelo felt toward fellow lefty artists such as Leonardo da Vinci and Raphael. In this case both Connors and McEnroe were too much the angry lefty for them to get on together. Part of this animosity may well have been because they each canceled the other's natural lefty advantage out.

6. Martina Navratilova is not the only talented left-hander in these pages who was gay. Others include Michelangelo, Leonardo and Alan Turing.

7. In his autobiography, McEnroe questions whether his temper tantrums on the court were more of a hindrance than an asset.

He argues that they were just as capable of ruining his game as that of his opponents, and that he would have rather not have had them if he could have helped it. McEnroe claims that for him the fear of losing was a more powerful motivator than the joy of winning, hence the element of self-loathing in his outbursts. In other respects, however, McEnroe's rage was natural, as was his freakish touch with shots such as the drop volley. Like Michelangelo, he was the product of a rage for perfection within himself. It seems that in many lefty geniuses, there is an inseparable connection between their brilliance and their rage, adding weight to the theory that lefties are formed by an exposure to an excess of testosterone in the womb. Certainly Navratilova, who as a child was often mistaken for a boy, also had problems with the self-destructive capacity of her own anger on the court, especially in the earlier part of her career.

A FAMILIAR IMAGE OF McENROE DISPUTING THE UMPIRE'S CALL DURING A CHAMPIONSHIP LAWN TENNIS MATCH AT WIMBLEDON.

JOHN McENROE
1959–

**INTUITIVE** McEnroe's touch play and career-long ability to surprise his opponents were the marks of an intuitive player, as were his emotionalism and capacity to get under their skins.

**VISUAL-SPATIAL ABILITY** McEnroe's unique shot angles, in particular, showed a superior visual-spatial mind at work.

**HOT-TEMPERED** Nicknamed Super Brat, McEnroe has one of the most famous tempers in left-handed history.

**ICONOCLASTIC** In many ways McEnroe brought the punk ethos to tennis. He took on the stuffy administrators of Wimbledon and won, while *The New York Times* once described him as "the worst advertisement for our system of values since Al Capone." He used his image as a rebel to make millions through an endorsement deal with Nike.

**FANTASIST** How else can McEnroe's post-tennis attempt to become a rock star guitarist be explained?

champion: contained, logical, remorseless. On the court he showed no sign of emotion. When he met with McEnroe in the 1980 Wimbledon Final, Borg had won the championship for the previous four years. McEnroe, on the other hand, was already becoming famous for his on-court explosions of rage. When he came on center court for the final he was booed by the crowd because of his bad behavior toward officials during his tense semi-final against fellow lefty and hot-head Jimmy Connors.

The quality of play, however, would soon stun the booers into silence. It was the first time McEnroe played Borg on grass and because of Borg's baseline game, he believed he had his measure. In the first set it seemed so. McEnroe, with his fast-reaction serve volley game, cleaned up 6–1. In the second, McEnroe was winning 5–4, with his serve to come, and starting to think he had climbed the mountain and was about to coast home. The idea appealed to him since he was exhausted, having beaten Connors in four sets the day before, and played his delayed doubles semi-final straight after. Borg, however, had other ideas. With McEnroe letting his foot off the pedal just a little, Borg found rhythm with his serve to win the set 7–5. For McEnroe, tennis was about controlling the inner voices of negativity as much as outdoing the opponent. Angry at himself for losing a set he thought he should have won, he proceeded to lose the next one 3–6. Worse still, in the fourth set he was broken by Borg and was down 3–5. If Borg won the next game, the match was over. Yet McEnroe dug deep and held his serve, saving a couple of match points in the process, before bringing the set to a tie-break by breaking Borg then holding serve again. This tie-break became the most famous tie-break in the history of Wimbledon. Lasting for over 20 minutes of supreme tension, McEnroe defended a further five match points before taking the set with a score of 18–16. At this stage, McEnroe was sure he had the game won. Borg, however, was relentless and McEnroe just couldn't break his serve in the final set which Borg won 8–6 to take the match and his fifth successive Wimbledon title.

While he may have lost arguably the greatest final in tennis history, McEnroe learned much from it and he won all the remaining three Grand Slam finals he played against Borg. In the epic five-setter, he had absorbed the enemy's game and now he knew how to conquer him. At the US Open that year, two months after Wimbledon, he beat Borg in another epic five-setter, in which there were tie-breaks in the first, second and third sets, after also defeating Connors and Ivan Lendl on the way through. Then at Wimbledon in 1981, he beat Borg in four sets, breaking his record 41 match-winning Wimbledon streak and denying him his sixth successive title. McEnroe then beat Borg in a relatively easy four-set game at the US Open, the last Grand Slam final the 11-time Grand Slam tournament winner would ever play in.

In a sense, McEnroe broke Borg. After losing the US Open in 1981, Borg never played in another Grand Slam event and, in 1982, he retired from the game at the young age of 25. McEnroe was bereft. While relationships between tennis players in the upper echelons of the game are often either indifferent or antipathetic, there was a real synergy between these rivals as if in their left versus right rivalry, each player completed what was missing in the other. As such, their rivalry was imbued with the utmost respect. In 2006 when Borg, having fallen into financial difficulties, decided to auction two of his Wimbledon trophies and one of the tennis racquets he'd used to win it, several players rang to ask him what the story was. It was McEnroe, however, according to sources close to Borg, who rang up and said, "What's up. Have you gone mad?" and was thus able to make Borg change his mind.

## McENROE STATISTICS

At 5 feet 11 inches, but weighing an average of only 165 pounds throughout his career, McEnroe preceded the bigger specimens dominating the court today. Yet his record speaks for itself. After turning pro in 1978, he won 869 of his 1,063 singles games and 530 of his 629 doubles games, despite playing on for five or six years past his evident peak. McEnroe's peak came in 1984 when he had a record of 82 wins against 3 defeats—a record unmatched by any player before or since. (Federer came closest in 2005 with a 81–3 win.) During his career, McEnroe won 77 singles tournaments and 78 doubles tournaments, an all-time record of 155 at the top level, for a total prize money of US$12,547,797. He was Number 1 in the world for a total of 170 weeks in his career. He also won seven Grand Slam singles tournaments—four US Opens and three Wimbledons; and nine in doubles—five Wimbledons and four US Opens. Unlike many of his contemporaries, McEnroe was sufficiently patriotic to play the Davis Cup, where he had a 59–10 record, and set US records for years played (12), ties (30), singles wins (41), and total wins in singles and doubles (59).

OPPOSITE: McENROE AND FELLOW LEFT-HANDED TENNIS GIANT, JIMMY CONNORS, WIMBLEDON, 1977.

PAGE 235: McENROE HAVING AN ON-COURT TANTRUM, FOLLOWING AN UMPIRE'S CALL AT WIMBLEDON, 1980.

# The Lefty White House Cluster

WHILE ONLY TEN PERCENT OF THE POPULATION IS LEFT-HANDEED, SIX OUT of the last eight American Presidents have been lefties, a remarkable statistic since the task of climbing to the top of the world's major democracy tends to necessitate some smoothing out of the more idiosyncratic lefty traits. The run began when Gerald Ford assumed the presidency in 1974, following the resignation of Richard Nixon in disgrace. When Ford inherited the Presidency, America was in crisis. He had to navigate the Watergate scandal, work out an exit strategy for the failed Vietnam War, and deal with the inflationary conditions instigated by the 1973 OPEC oil crisis. By the time he lost narrowly to Carter, the first two problems had largely been solved. After one term tainted by the Iran hostage crisis, Carter lost in a landslide to left-handed Californian former actor, Ronald Reagan. The rise of the left-handed Presidents saw the decline of left-wing politics in the world. America's power increased dramatically under Reagan, through the gradual collapse of the Soviet Empire. After two terms, Reagan was succeeded by his left-handed Vice-President, George Bush, a former World War Two fighter pilot, Texas oilman, and head of the CIA. Bush was President in 1989 when the Berlin Wall came down, presided over victory in the First Gulf War and consolidated America's new status as the world's only genuine superpower. However, he fell victim to the fluctuations of the economic cycle and lost after one term, to the charismatic, saxophone playing, former Governor of Arkansas and fellow left-hander Bill Clinton. With relative peace on the international front, Clinton presided over two terms of prosperity, propelled by the dot-com boom of the nineties. There are doubts as to whether America benefitted from its shift back to the right during the two terms of George W. Bush. Certainly the legacy of the world financial crisis bequeathed to Obama means that his presidency in addition to its symbolic significance will be a particularly difficult one as he tries to chart a course to bring the United States through the worst economic crisis since the Great Depression.

CLOCKWISE FROM TOP LEFT:
GERALD FORD, 38TH US PRESIDENT
FROM 1974–77; RONALD REAGAN,
40TH US PRESIDENT FROM 1981–89;
GEORGE H. W. BUSH, 41ST
US PRESIDENT FROM 1989–93;
BILL CLINTON, 42ND US PRESIDENT
FROM 1993–2001; BARACK OBAMA,
44TH US PRESIDENT FROM 2009.

**GERALD FORD** After Richard Nixon sullied the American Presidency, Gerald Ford was the man who got the job, in 1974, of trying to clean it up. A man universally known for his negotiating skills and rare political honesty, he tried to undo the damage Nixon had done and was also responsible for extricating the last American troops from Vietnam. Born in Nebraska, but raised in Michigan, Ford was the political embodiment of the upright values of America's midwest. They weren't sufficient, however, to get him elected. Faced with the fallout from his pardoning of Nixon and deteriorating economic circumstances, he narrowly failed to be elected in the Presidential race of 1976.

One of the most intriguing things about the great lefty cluster of US Presidents is that they all came from homes where either violence or alcoholism was a presence. Whether this is related to the statistics for left-handers having hot tempers, or being vulnerable to addiction, is unknown, since the handedness of their parents has not been recorded. In Ford's case the violence, in the form of his biological father, was expunged from the house before the son was really aware of it. Ford's mother, Dorothy, had married Lesley Lynch King, a wool trader and wife-beater. Sixteen days after the birth of Ford, the couple separated after King threatened to kill his wife, the baby and his nanny with a butcher's knife. Ford and his mother moved to Grand Rapids, Michigan, where her parents lived. Soon after, she met and married Gerald Rudolff Ford, a salesman in a paint and varnish company, who Ford believed was his real father until he was 17 years old.

As a child, Ford had a fierce temper and was prone to tantrums. His mom was concerned that he had inherited his father's violent streak and determined to teach him control. When he got angry, she tried to reason with him, or sent him to his room to cool off. This early taming of his temper was central to the kind of politician Ford became; someone whose talents lay in building bridges, negotiation and calming stormy waters.

Ford's most conspicuous talents as a youth were on the sporting field. He is arguably the best athlete ever to become American President. After graduating from high school, he won a football scholarship to the University of Michigan and on graduating he was offered contracts to play professionally with the Chicago Bears and Green Bay Packers. He usually played center or linebacker, two positions which demanded strategical intelligence and visual-spatial skills. Ford declined offers to become a professional footballer in favor of going to Yale, where he worked as a football and boxing coach while studying law.

During World War II, Ford joined the navy, where his position as assistant navigator on the aircraft carrier USS *Monterey* also utilized his superior visual-spatial skills.

After becoming active in Grand Rapids Republican politics, Ford was elected to the US House of Representatives in 1949. He remained there until 1973 until events catapulted him first to the Vice-Presidency then the

## GERALD FORD
## 1913–2006

**INTUITIVE** All successful politicians need to have some intuitive know-how, an ability to see what those around them are thinking and be able to think on their feet. Ford had these talents but they don't appear to have been exceptional.

**EMPATHETIC** Much of Ford's personality was dedicated to keeping people happy, and he was able to empathize with people in order to achieve political compromises and form consensus without getting too many people off-side.

**VISUAL-SPATIAL ABILITY** Not so much in terms of Ford's political career, but this quality was definitely evident in his sporting and naval careers.

**HOT-TEMPERED** Ford inherited his father's bad temper, but it was trained out of him by his mother.

**FANTASIST** Did Ford really think the public would accept him letting Nixon off?

OPPOSITE: AFTER BEING THE CAPTAIN OF THE HIGH SCHOOL FOOTBALL TEAM, FORD WENT ON TO STAR IN THE UNIVERSITY OF MICHIGAN TEAM AS LINEBACKER AND CENTER. FORD'S SPORTING PROWESS WAS AT ODDS WITH THE PRESIDENT'S LATER REPUTATION FOR CLUMSINESS.

## RONALD REAGAN
### 1911–2004

**INTUITIVE** Reagan had the actor's intuition of knowing how to present himself and his cause to an audience.

**EMPATHETIC** Reagan's folksy fatherly political persona made him attractive to the American people.

**LATERAL THINKING** Reagan possessed the skills for adaptation and transformation, which have seen many left-handers become thespians.

**ICONOCLASTIC** Reagan was the first divorced President. Also, the timing of his switch from Democrat to Republican during the Kennedy era illustrated his ability to disregard the benefits of conformity in quest of his own truths.

**SELF-TAUGHT** Although Reagan studied economics at college, he learned most of the economics of his "Reaganomics" through his reading in the 1960s. Like many left-handers, he was also strong on learning from experience.

**FANTASIST** Reagan sold a dream of America as the "shining city" of liberty and freedom. Like any great salesman, he believed his story.

OPPOSITE: AFTER HE LEFT COLLEGE IN 1932 RONALD REAGAN BECAME A RADIO SPORTS ANNOUNCER, WORKING FOR WARNER BROS FOR SEVEN YEARS. DURING THE HEIGHT OF THE DEPRESSION, HE WAS EARNING $75 PER WEEK.

Presidency. Unlike many of the left-handers in this book, whose success is defined by their stubborn singularity and ability to stand up against status quo, Ford was a consensus kind of guy, known for his empathetic skills as a reconciler and negotiator rather than any bold legislative strokes. It was his reputation for not rocking the boat which saw him foisted upon Nixon as Vice-President by Congress, when Spiro Agnew resigned after being charged with tax evasion and money laundering.

When Nixon was forced to resign over the Watergate tapes on August 9, 1974, Ford was thrown into the Presidency at a time when its reputation had been severely damaged. Ford did his best to mend fences. His granting of a presidential pardon to Nixon, before there was even a trial, caused a scandal, and it was speculated that Ford and Nixon had done a deal. They hadn't. Ford's reasoning was that by pardoning Nixon, the damage to the office of the Presidency would be minimized. Yet the controversy that his pardon created, along with the economic problem of stagflation, was pivotal in Ford losing the 1976 election to Jimmy Carter.

Ford was not your typical lefty by virtue of his seeming normality. Yet in the conspicuous effort of a career devoted toward being a peace-maker, there was something of the left-handed insecurity of being an outsider trying to fit in. Some great lefties manage this by acquiring the authority to make the world fit in with them. This is harder to do in a democratic system and it probably wasn't Ford's way at any rate. He died on Boxing Day, 2006, at the ripe old age of 93.

**RONALD REAGAN** Although he got to the Presidency via Hollywood, in many ways Reagan was almost the embodiment of the log cabin myth. Born in a flat on top of a bank in an Illinois village, his father was a shoe salesman and the family moved around often before they settled in the town of Dixon, Illinois, when Reagan was nine. Although Reagan often tapped into the sentimental fantasy of small-town American life, romanticizing his childhood and the values it apparently taught him, his childhood wasn't always easy. His father was frequently out of work, and prone to getting on the sauce—another case where a left-handed President overcame either the violence or alcoholism in their genes.

At Dixon High, Reagan discovered an ability for storytelling and acting which would open his mind to a larger world and also give him his first taste of how the power of speech can transform it. Upon graduating from high school, he attended Eureka College, a small private college in a town not far from his home, where he majored in economics and sociology. Following college, Reagan began to work in radio. His love of sports and skill for story-telling combined when, between 1932 and 1937, he became baseball announcer for the WHO station based in Des Moines, Iowa. From a telegraph report that showed only the bare bones of the game, Reagan's job was to concoct the story of what was happening out on the pitch. Apparently his skills with this were such that, when the line went down during a game one

## LEFTY LINKS

1. At the time of writing it appears possible that the Presidency will once again move to the left in the elections of 2008. With the Republicans in trouble, one of the leading Democrat contenders, Barack Obama, is also a lefty. For the Republicans, Senator John McCain happens to be a lefty too.

2. There is some precedent for an all-lefty Presidential race. In the 1992 Presidential Election all three candidates were lefties: George H. W. Bush, Bill Clinton and independent Texan billionaire Ross Perot. All in all, seven of the 43 (or 16 percent) of the Presidents of the United States have been left-handed, a higher proportion than the 10 percent of left-handers in the population. This supports the theory that there are proportionally more left-handers at the high end of the achievement spectrum. The other three are 20th President James Garfield (1831–81), who was assassinated only six months into the job; 31st President Herbert Hoover (1874–1964) who was President between 1929–1933 during the Great Depression; and Harry S. Truman (1884–1972) who became President in 1945 on the death of F. D. Roosevelt, and held on for a second term with an upset election win in 1948.

3. The current cluster of left-handed Presidents is particularly interesting given the relative dearth of famous left-handed politicians in other countries. Perhaps this is because government favors people who belong to majorities. However there are notable exceptions: India's founding President, Mahatma Gandhi, Cuban leader Fidel Castro, Israel's fiery former Prime Minister, Benjamin Netanyahu, current Israeli PM Ehud Ohlmert, US Christian right-winger Pat Robertson, Ireland's long-serving leader, Bertie O'Hearn, Australian Foreign Minister Alexander Downer, Japan's volatile right-wing Mayor of Tokyo Ishihara Shintaro, and F. W. De Klerk who, as President of South Africa, helped bring about the end of the apartheid era. Only one British Prime Minister, James Callaghan, has been left-handed. Winston Churchill has often been credited with being a left-hander, yet this is not true, though he does have many left-handed traits and could possibly be a switched lefty.

day, he made up a sequence of the game composed entirely of batters hitting fouls (to keep the score static) until the telegraph feed resumed.

In 1937, Reagan took a successful screen test with Warner Brothers Pictures and his movie career began as a contract actor. If not quite an A-grade star, he was still a well-known leading man in the pre-war era.

Reagan's personal life demonstrated the gap between Hollywood values and mainstream America at that time. In 1940, he married actress Jane Wyman, who had been his leading lady in a number of films. They had a daughter, adopted a son, then had another daughter who died in infancy. In 1948, they divorced. Four years later Reagan married another actress, Nancy Davis. It was a meeting of soulmates and she remained his partner until death. Nonetheless, Reagan is somewhat iconoclastic, given his conservative politics, in that he remains the only President of the United States to have ever been divorced.

During the war, Reagan volunteered for active service but was deemed unfit because of problems with his eyes. After the war, his career shifted toward politics, when he became President of the Screen Actors Guild (SAG), effectively a union leader. At this stage in his life, Reagan was a self-described "hemophiliac liberal."

The strongest influence in Reagan's eventual shift from being a Democrat to a Republican was communism. Reagan was a libertarian, a common stance for lefties forced to live with the tyranny of the majority. It was a position strengthened by his growing antipathy to the collective threat of communism. In his role as President of the Screen Actor's Guild, Reagan testified against some fellow actors to Senator McCarthy's Commission on UnAmerican Activities, and was also a source for the FBI. During the fifties, while still a Democrat, he supported both Eisenhower and Nixon. He also returned to his college major, economics, and became a convert to free market theories advocated by libertarian thinkers such as Friedrich Hayek. Blessed with the left-handed capacity for adaptation and transformation which had graced his acting career, his political conversion coincided with a new job as a television host for a show funded by General Electric.

Reagan's film career ended in 1964 with *The Killers*. Aided by a beneficial land deal organized by Wasserman, Reagan achieved sufficient financial independence to stand for public office. In 1966, he became California Governor, froze hiring and balanced the budget. He also showed an illiberal streak tinged with the ruthlessness of the lefty conqueror in his prepared-ness to use violence to subdue anti-Vietnam protests.

After two terms as Governor, Reagan stood as a conservative against the more moderate Ford in the race for the Republican nomination for the 1976 Presidential elections. He lost this one but won the nomination in 1980 and defeated Jimmy Carter easily. In 1984, he defeated Walter Mondale in a landslide, winning 49 out of 50 states.

As President, Reagan's political attitude was classically liberal: "The Founding Fathers knew a government can't control the economy without controlling people. And they knew when a government set out to do that, it must use force and coercion to achieve its purpose. So we have come to a time for choosing." In effect he chose both. While his "Reaganomics" of cutting taxes and deregulating the domestic economy helped America recover from the recession of the seventies, his expenditure on defense in staring down the crumbling Soviet empire helped America change from being the world's highest creditor nation at the beginning of his Presidency, to the highest debtor nation by its end. Deregulation also fueled the activities of the financially unscrupulous and the era was marked by controversies such as the Savings and Loans Scandal, the yuppy fever of the Wall Street boom and security scandals such as Contragate, which sanctioned covert American involvement in the drug and gun trade to help fund rebels against the leftist regime in Nicaragua.

Undoubtedly Reagan's major achievement was presiding over the largely peaceful disintegration of the communist bloc. By the time he handed over the Presidency to George Bush, communism, which Reagan abhorred, was finished. It was a victory that Reagan achieved largely through rhetorical means. The skills he had learned as an actor proved invaluable. As Margaret Thatcher said, "He took words and sent them out to fight for us."

**GEORGE BUSH** If Ford and Reagan came from relatively lowly backgrounds, George H. W. Bush entered the world as an Eastern States blueblood. His father was Prescott Bush—Yale graduate, wealthy merchant banker and US Senator, and his mother's father, Bert Walker, was an old-school robber baron who made his millions on Wall Street largely through insider trading. Perhaps the only quality of Bush's childhood that he shared with Ford, Reagan and Clinton was a problematic father. Despite his superficial success and the millions he made, Prescott Bush was a drunk and prone to over-application of the strap in the pursuit of disciplined children.

From an early age, Bush proved a natural leader. At his exclusive prep school, he was President of his senior year class and captain of the baseball and soccer teams. When he graduated in 1942, he joined the Navy and became a pilot, a job whose three-dimensional navigation demands enhanced visual-spatial skills. In the war, he demonstrated the conspicuous bravery seen in lefty warriors such as Alexander, Caesar, Napoleon and Joan of Arc. In 1944, he was on a raid to bomb installations on a Japanese island when his plane came under heavy anti-aircraft fire. Bush's plane was hit and half his crew killed. Despite the fact that his engine was on fire, Bush continued to head for the target. When he reached it, he dropped his payload of bombs before bailing out and parachuting into the ocean where he was rescued by a submarine four hours later. His other crewmate's parachute had failed to open and Bush was the only survivor. For his bravery, he was awarded the Distinguished Flying Cross, America's highest aerial medal.

With the war over, Bush got married then went to college. He continued the family's Ivy League tradition of attending Yale. Like Ford he was a

## GEORGE BUSH
## 1924–

**VISUAL-SPATIAL ABILITY**
This shows in Bush's flying and baseball prowess, yet also in his predilection for the chess of geo-political strategy.

**LATERAL THINKING** As a youngster, Bush was renowned for his practical jokes, while his rise to the top had some unusual diversions. His time in the spy game often involved the transformative skills of making one thing appear like another, an example of which was his involvement in the extremely murky Iran Contra affair, which saw the CIA illegally selling weapons to Iran to fund right-wing guerillas in Nicaragua.

**EXPERIMENTAL** Instead of entering Wall Street, Bush took the risk of moving to Texas, joining the oil industry and eventually starting his own company.

**FANTASIST** Bush has shown a life-long love for the behind-the-scenes, cloak and dagger stuff of the CIA.

OPPOSITE: FOR HEROIC ACTIONS IN THE AIR FORCE DURING WORLD WAR II, GEORGE BUSH WAS AWARDED THE DISTINGUISHED FLYING CROSS.

seriously good sportsman. As a left-handed first baseman, he was not only captain of the Yale team, but played in the first and second College World Series, where his team were consecutive runners-up, the only two times Yale has ever made it to the final.

When Bush graduated from Yale, like Reagan with a degree in economics, he turned down offers to work with his father and grandfather's firms for a chance to work in the developing oil industry. He got a job with a subsidiary of Dresser Industries, a company where his father was a long-standing member of the board. In 1953, he started Zapata Oil with two business partners. By the end of the 1950s all of them were millionaires. Bush also allowed the CIA to use Zapata's off-shore assets as a staging point for raids into Cuba. Even before Bush became Director of the CIA, there seems to have been a clear penchant for the cloak and dagger stuff.

Bush first campaigned for a Texan seat in the US Senate in 1964, but lost in a battle which saw him derided as "a tool of the eastern kingmakers." In 1966, he was elected to the House of Representatives and proved the value of his connections by being appointed almost immediately to the Committee of Ways and Means. With its authority over tax and revenue, it is the most powerful committee in the House of Representatives and it was unusual for such an inexperienced politician to get the nod. After being re-elected to Congress in 1968, Bush stood for the senate in 1970 and lost again. As a consolation, Nixon appointed him Ambassador to the United Nations, then in the crucial role as Special Envoy to China. When Gerald Ford became President, he appointed Bush as Director of the CIA, where he proved not to be the reforming outsider that he was made out to be. These jobs reveal Bush's particular interest in the mechanics of big picture, geo-political strategy, a kind of thinking that involves abstracted utilization of the kinds of visual-spatial skills that made someone like Napoleon such a brilliant general.

In 1980, Bush became Reagan's running mate after Reagan defeated him for the presidential nomination, illustrating Bush's diplomatic skills. As with Ford and Rockefeller it was a double lefty team. He served two terms as Vice-President, then in 1988 won the Republican nomination and was elected President just in time for the Berlin Wall to fall. It was a Presidency concentrated on foreign policy, where Bush's skills of diplomacy, geo-political nous, and CIA insider knowledge proved invaluable. However, following the economic boom of the Reagan era, the end of the eighties saw America slide into recession. As a conspicuous blueblood, Bush couldn't help but look out of touch with the American people. He lacked Reagan's genius for generating the effect of empathy and it cost him. His perceived failure to finish the First Gulf War properly by killing Saddam Hussein, who as CIA Director he had supported, also damaged his chances for re-election, as did his backpedaling on his "no new taxes" election pledge. In 1993, he handed over the Presidency to his fellow lefty, Bill Clinton.

**BILL CLINTON** Of all the left-handed Presidents surveyed here, Bill Clinton had the toughest background. His biological father, William Blythe, was a traveling salesman who was married four times (including to a pair of sisters) by the time he was 25. He was killed in a car crash three months before Clinton was born. When Clinton was four, his mother married Roger Clinton, a used car dealer in Hot Springs, Arkansas. If his real father was a philanderer, his stepfather was a violent alcoholic who used to abuse Clinton's mother and his half-brother.

As a kid, Clinton was into playing the saxophone and considered becoming a pro. However, he realized early that, while he was good, he was probably never going to be great. Unlike many left-handers in this book, but like all his fellow lefty Presidents, Clinton excelled academically. Education was his chance at escaping from uninspiring family circumstances. In high school, he was a delegate to Boys Nation, a scheme where two of the best students from each state go to Washington DC to learn about government. While Clinton was there he met President John Kennedy. By the time he came home he'd decided on politics for his career.

Clinton won scholarships to Georgetown University, Washington, where he studied Foreign Service before winning a coveted Rhodes Scholarship to Oxford in 1968, where he joined the educated elites of his generation in toking on joints, protesting against the Vietnam War and, less conventionally for an American, playing rugby. Like his predecessor, George Bush, Clinton headed a Presidency with a strong foreign policy emphasis, which might be related to his left-handed facility for difference and adaptation. Clinton is also one of few American Presidents to have spent time living abroad before entering politics.

Like Ford and Bush, Clinton went to Yale, where he studied law, graduating in 1973, before returning to Arkansas to begin his political career. In 1978, aged 32, Clinton became the youngest Governor in the country. Having benefited from his own education he put money into making educational opportunities available for all. He lost his re-election campaign in 1980, but showed tenacity and won the job back in 1982 and held onto it until resigning it to contest the Presidency in 1992.

Clinton won the 1992 elections and in 1996 became the first Democratic President to be re-elected since Franklin D. Roosevelt. Clinton's time as President was a period of great prosperity in America. He shared with Reagan an empathetic quality that Bush had lacked. They both used their charm to make their way from the boondocks to the center of the nation. Both had the skillset of great actors, including the ability to narrate fiction with utter conviction. According to some political commentators, Clinton's greatest skill was his ability to adapt his ideas to whatever the electorate was thinking. Unfortunately, his second term was mired in the Monica Lewinsky scandal and the subsequent witch hunt that led to his impeachment. Since leaving politics, Clinton remains an important presence in global issues.

**BILL CLINTON 1946–**

**EMPATHETIC** Clinton is one of the most charismatic men to ever grace the stage of American politics. His charm is famous for its quality of total attention, making a person feel like he or she is the only one alive at that given point in time.

**LATERAL THINKING** In his Presidency and subsequently, Clinton has strongly advocated multi-lateral solutions to the more intractable political problems of international relations.

**HOT-TEMPERED** Was reported by his aide George Stephanopoulos as responding to the Somalian crisis by saying, "We're not inflicting pain on these fuckers. When people kill us, they should be killed in greater numbers. I believe in killing people who try to hurt you. And I can't believe we're being pushed around by these two-bit pricks."

**EXPERIMENTAL** Clinton toked but didn't inhale.

**FANTASIST** Clinton was liberal with the truth, often to comic effect, such as classifying oral sex as belonging outside the field of sexual relations.

OPPOSITE: THE YOUNG BILL CLINTON VISITED WASHINGTON IN 1963, AS A BOYS NATION SENATOR, AND MET PRESIDENT KENNEDY.

## BARACK OBAMA
## 1961–

**INTUITIVE** His multi-cultural background has enhanced his left-handed intuitive abilities since his upbringing necessitated reading the characters of a wide variety of people from a young age.

**EMPATHETIC** In his career as a community organizer in Altgeld on the southside of Chicago, he showed an ability to get close to the people he worked with, so much so that he clashed with his boss, Marty Kaufman who thought Obama's empathy might lead to him burning out.

**LATERAL THINKING** This is perhaps a product of his upbringing where he has learned to juggle conflicting cultures and influences and adapt to new circumstances. There is a sense of flexibility in his intellect that is not always found in American presidents. His stance against the Iraq War against the tide is one example of lateral thinking in his politics.

**SOLITARY** Effectively an only child, he was also often out of place in the world and forced to rely on his own resources. Once he finished college he increasingly showed a preference for studying at home with his books rather than carousing with colleagues and friends.

**ICONOCLASTIC** Just by becoming the first African-American President, he is arguably the most iconoclastic of all. In his early term he has pushed to make a break on a number of policy fronts, such as climate change and the withdrawal of American troops from Iraq.

**EXPERIMENTAL** While probably not the first American President to dabble in illicit substances, Obama is the first to openly admit to it. His career path also shows the pragmatic testing of conditions which is often found in left-handers of an experimental bent. Rather than an idealist he often says he is interested in what works.

## BARACK OBAMA

While the election of Barack Obama as American President in 2008 has the retrospective aura of destiny being fulfilled, for most of his life the most powerful job in the world was a long way away. Obama's Mom, Stanley Ann Dunham, was born in Kansas in the mid-west but moved to Hawaii with her parents, while his father, Barack Obama Sr, was from the Luo tribe in Kenya. The two met while they were both students at the East-West Centre of the University of Hawaii. The marriage, however, didn't last and by the time young Barack was two his parents had separated. Obama senior abandoned his young family to take up doctoral studies at Harvard, then returned to Kenya, where his abilities were self-sabotaged by arrogance and an inability to play politics. Father and son would only meet one more time (in 1971), before Obama senior died in a car crash in 1982.

Obama's cross-cultural upbringing was central to the development of his character. Of all the states in America, Hawaii was perhaps the least segregated. Having divorced Obama's Dad, his Mom started going out with an Indonesian exchange student, Lolo Soetoro. In 1967, Obama, his Mom and Soetoro moved to the outskirts of Djakarta. In his autobiography *Dreams From My Father*, Obama writes of this time as a formative experience where he learned how harsh the world could be. He also went to a local *bahasa* (the language of Indonesia) speaking school, where he studied the Islamic religion. Such experiences undoubtedly enhanced the left-hander's native capacity for adapting to a world into which they don't fit.

The marriage between Soetoro and Obama's Mom did not work out well. Like Obama's real father, Soetoro fell foul of the political establishment. His ambitions were cruelled and he hit the bottle. Against the background of a deteriorating marriage, when he was ten years old, Obama's Mom decided to send him to live in Hawaii with her parents so he could get a good education. Obama won entry to the prestigious Punahou Academy, where he was one of only three black students in his year. Once again he had to use his lefty adaptability to acclimatise to new conditions. At Punahou he was also exposed to American-style racism for the first time. Yet the love of his white Mom and grandparents meant that he never became a reactionary racist himself. He conquered his new conditions and graduated with Honors in 1979.

Like many people, Obama's first years as a college student were largely spent slacking until he transferred to Columbia University for his final years. Upon graduating, he decided to become a community organizer. It took a while to find a job and Obama first worked as a corporate writer before he finally landed work with Marty Kaufman, a veteran organizer working to save manufacturing jobs in Chicago. After learning the ropes, Obama ended up devoting his organizing energies in the ghetto district of Altgeld in Southside Chicago where he developed a strong empathy for the residents he worked with. His life again showed signs of the lefty solitary. During this time, he also visited relatives in Kenya for the first time, which helped to fill out many of the questions he had about his paternal heritage, and also gave him another cultural perspective from which he could read the world.

In his Southside organising days, Obama learned much about the structure of power, and in order to consolidate this knowledge, he decided to apply for Harvard Law School to put himself in a position where he could make social change happen. At Harvard, his star shone. He gained a summer associateship at the prestigious Chicago law firm, Sidley and Austin, where he took a shine to his mentor, Michelle Robinson, who later became his wife. In 1995 he became the first African-American President of the Harvard Law Review. The world was his oyster, but instead of taking up a lucrative gig in the corporate world, he showed fidelity to his ideals by returning to community organising in Chicago. It was a somewhat iconoclastic decision perhaps, but one spurred by intuition and an unconventional sense of destiny which matched his unconventional origins.

After his return to Chicago, Obama became increasingly involved in party politics and in 1997 he was elected Democrat senator to the Illinois senate. In 1999, he ran for a Democrat seat in the US Congress but lost in the primaries to a former Black Panther activist. The defeat left him broke. Soon after, 9/11 left him wondering whether anyone with his name could ever be electable. However, his confidence returned and in 2002 he decided to run for the US Senate. Against the odds, he won the Democratic primary. Obama's star continued to rise when Democratic president nominee, John Kerry, asked him to deliver the keynote address at the Democratic National Convention. Obama delivered his brilliant Audacity of Hope speech, which marked him as brilliant and persuasive speaker. It was a speech which argued for unity over the schisms in American culture, something Obama was uniquely qualified to do as he was the unified embodiment of so many of these tensions. In the election he defeated the Republican candidate to become only the fifth African American US Senator.

It was a meteoric rise, but of course it wasn't over. In 2007, Obama announced his candidacy for President. Against him were the talented and formidably connected Hillary Clinton and John Edwards, John Kerry's vice-presidential running mate in the 2004 Presidential election. However, with the war in Iraq having stagnated, there were signs that the electorate was willing to consider an outsider as President, something mirrored in the Republican primaries where left-handed maverick John McCain won. Obama overcame the odds in a fiercely fought battle against Hillary Clinton. The actual election was somewhat easier. The sub-prime crisis and Iraq turned George W. Bush into a lame-duck president during the last year of his final term, and made it extremely difficult for McCain to gain momentum. Obama ran an astute and measured campaign. In November 2008, he won the election with 69 million votes to McCain's 59 million, winning 365 of the electoral college votes to McCain's 173. The left's lefty had beaten the right's. Of course, Obama has inherited difficult times to govern in, but it may be just the chance for an out of the box lefty thinker with a heightened cultural awareness to provide new solutions to some of the United States's social and structural problems.

# Further reading

Ackroyd, Peter, *Brief Lives: Newton*, Chatto and Windus, 2006

Adams, Tim, *Being John McEnroe*, Yellow Jersey Press, 2004

Arnstein, Walter L., *Queen Victoria*, Palgrave Macmillan, 2003

Bakewell, Michael, *Lewis Carroll: A Biography*, William Heinemann, 1996

Blue, Adrianne, *Martina Unauthorized*, Gollancz, 1995

Bragg, Melvyn, *On Giants' Shoulders: Great Scientists and their Discoveries from Archimedes to DNA*, Hodder and Stoughton, 1998

Brunskill, Ian (ed.), *Great Lives: A Century in Obituaries*, Times Books, 2005

Calder, Angus, *Gods, Mongrels and Demons, 101 Brief but Essential Lives*, Bloomsbury, 2003

Carroll, Lewis, *Alice's Adventures in Wonderland, Through the Looking-Glass*, and *The Hunting of the Snark*, Bodley Head, 1974

Cohen, Morton N., *Lewis Carroll: A Biography*, Macmillan, 1995

Collier, Peter and Horowitz, David, *The Fords: An American Epic*, Encounter Books, 2002

Coren, Stanley, *The Left-Hander Syndrome*, The Free Press, 1992

Crossen, Cynthia, *The Rich and How They Got That Way*, Crown Publishers, 2000

Dry, Sarah, *Curie*, Haus Publishing, 2003

Fincher, Jack, *Lefties: The Origins and Consequences of Being Left-handed*, Barnes & Noble, 1977

Freedberg, S. J., *Painting in Italy 1500–1600*, Pelican, 1990

Gardner, Howard, *Creative Minds*, Basic Books, 1993

Gergel, Tania (ed.), *Alexander: Selected Texts from Arrian, Curtius and Plutarch*, Penguin, 2005

Gleick, James, *Isaac Newton*, Pantheon, 2003

Goffen, Rona, *Renaissance Rivals: Michelangelo, Leonardo, Raphael, Titian*, Yale University Press, 2002

Gordon, Mary, *Joan Of Arc*, Penguin, 2000

Hodges, Andrew, *Alan Turing: The Enigma*, Simon and Schuster, 1983

Hollingdale, R. J., *Nietzsche: The Man and His Philosophy*, Cambridge University Press, 1999

Kemp, Martin, *Leonardo*, Oxford University Press, 2004

Lamb, Brian, *Booknotes Life Stories: Notable Biographers On the People Who Shaped America*, Three Rivers Press, 1999

Lucie-Smith, Edward, *Joan of Arc*, Allen Lane, 1976

Lynn, Kenneth S., *Charlie Chaplin and his Times*, Simon and Schuster, 1997

McEnroe, John, *Serious*, Little Brown, 2002

McManus, Chris, *Right Hand, Left Hand*, Phoenix, 2003

Menu, Bernadette, *Ramesses the Great: Warrior and Builder*, New Horizons, 1999

Miles, Barry, *Many Years From Now*, Vintage-Random House, 1998

Montville, Leigh, *The Big Bam: The Life and Times of Babe Ruth*, Doubleday, 2006

Nicholl, Charles, *Leonardo da Vinci: Flights of the Mind*, Viking, 2004

Orga, Ates, *Beethoven: His Life and Times*, Midas Books, 1978

Quinn, Susan, *Marie Curie: A Life*, William Heinemann, 1995

Shepherd, Rowena and Rupert, *1000 Symbols*, Thames and Hudson, 2002

Sofri, Gianni, *Gandhi and India*, Windrush Press, 1999

Strachey, Lytton, *Queen Victoria*, Chatto & Windus, 1922

Twain, Mark, *The Adventures of Huckleberry Finn*, Penguin, 1966

Twain, Mark, *The Adventures of Tom Sawyer*, Penguin, 1986

Tyldesley, Joyce, *Ramesses: Egypt's Greatest Pharaoh*, Penguin 2001

Vasari, Giorgio, *Lives of the Painters, Sculptors and Architects*, translated by Gaston de Vere, Everyman, 1996

Wallace, James, *Hard Drive: Bill Gates and the Making of the Microsoft Empire*, HarperCollins, 1993

West, Thomas G., *In the Mind's Eye: Visual Thinkers, Gifted People With Dyslexia and Other Learning Difficulties, Computer Images and the Ironies of Creativity*, Prometheus Books, 1991

Wolman, David, *A Left-Hand Turn Around the World: Chasing the Mystery and Meaning of All Things Southpaw*, Da Capo Press, 2005

Woodcock, George, *Gandhi*, Fontana, 1972

Wright, Ed, *Celebrity Family Trees: The World's Most Celebrated and Scandalous Dynasties*, Pier 9, 2006

Wullschläger, Jackie, *Inventing Wonderland*, Methuen, 1995

Wyn Jones, David, *The Life of Beethoven*, Cambridge University Press, 1998

Ziff, Larzer, *Mark Twain*, Oxford University Press, 2004

# Index